Reviews

"Suzanne's book is a timely, grounded, and most importantly a journey of self-discovery of unconditional love for her son. It combines research, clinical evidence and social and historical context, the book provider a rich tapestry of discovering gender along the spectrum of humanity. I would encourage anyone who wants to learn and embrace gender in its many forms, to read and go on a journey of love and compassion."

–Devan Nambiar, Founder and CEO,
Global Health Integrative Science

"If you worry that your questions about gender may cause some hurt, here is a clear, helpful, and powerful guide to being more open, accepting, and respectful."

–Mark Bowden, author "Winning Body Language" and
"TRUTH & LIES: What People Are *Really* Thinking"

"As a cis Human Resources professional, I thought I had a solid understanding of diversity and inclusion and its importance in our lives and workplaces. However, this insightful, engaging book opened up a whole new world to me. In a short period of time I had a new appreciation for our trans population and the difficult journey they travel. Thank you for this thoughtful and educational book that will assist me in both my career and in my personal life."

–Laini Torgerson, Chartered Professional
in Human Resources, Alberta

"*When Gender is in Question* is a non-threatening look at what is a threatening topic for many people: how we and our relationships are defined by gender. Whether you're thinking about your own gender identity, or being asked to understand someone else's, you'll find this book offers answers and invites the right questions.

Without preaching or pulling punches, it takes the reader through gender diversity's many aspects and intricacies, information, and misinformation like a helpful conversation with trusted friends. Combining the real-life perspectives of a trans man and his parent, and a gender specialist psychotherapist, *When Gender is in Question* speaks to everyone, and says things that everyone should hear."

–Peter Bruer, Senior Manager, Conflict Resolution & Training, St. Stephen's Community House, Toronto

"This book is a comprehensive "beginner's" guide, addressing questions and confusions that many of us have faced while wanting to be supportive to people whose dilemmas we do not ourselves completely comprehend. At the same time, the personal commentaries provided by members of the trans community lead us past understanding to empathy. For many of us, their struggle for authenticity has parallels to our own. This book helps us understand this very human struggle and how to be most human in solidarity."

–Dr. Peter Eliot Weiss, Associate Professor, Engineering Communication Program, University of Toronto

"This book is an absolute must-read for every HR professionals in every organization. More broadly, it's for every human being who is interested in a deeper understanding of themselves and others, both including and beyond questions of gender. Skyler Hagen's Forward to the book is one of the sweetest short essays on being and becoming I have ever read ... even *if* gender was not the central question! The authors bring clarity and wisdom to a subject that is complex, heavy, and confusing for many and they make it understandable, digestible, and acceptable."

–Mark Issacs, President, GS Research

"*When Gender is in Question* is a timely book for transgender people and their families. It is about a personal and familial journey of love and acceptance. Each chapter is filled with insight, honesty, and respect. It is a much-needed resource."

–Rev. Andrew Holmes, Ordained Minister, and social worker

"This book is a wonderful primer on understanding gender and what it means to transition from one gender to another. Suzanne provides the reader with three valuable perspectives: her own as the mother of a trans son, her child's insights of transitioning from female to male, and helpful medical information from a renowned gender specialist psychotherapist. After reading this book, I understand the topic so much more. Everyone should read this book."

–Carole Kelson, retired teacher

When
Gender
is In
Question

To Carmen
with love
& friendship

Suzmu

June/23

 FriesenPress

Suite 300 - 990 Fort St
Victoria, BC, V8V 3K2
Canada

www.friesenpress.com

ISBN
978-1-5255-7414-6 (Hardcover)
978-1-5255-7415-3 (Paperback)
978-1-5255-7416-0 (eBook)

1. FAMILY & RELATIONSHIPS, LGBT

Distributed to the trade by The Ingram Book Company

When Gender is In Question

A Guide to Understanding

Suzanne Sherkin with
Dr. Helma Seidl, PhD, MSW,
RSW, Psychotherapist,
and **Skyler Hagen**

DEDICATION

To Hugh for embracing change,
to Lauren for being a rock of support,
and to Sky for honouring your wisdom.

BEYOND THE WI

Mary Elizabeth

We are born to be

broken
open

again and again

a chance a hope

a glimpse of all there is.

An excerpt from the forthcoming book of a
narrative poem entitled, "Beyond the Wilds of Lila,"
by poet Mary Elizabeth Grace

TABLE OF CONTENTS

Foreword
by Skyler Hagen

When my mom first told me that she wanted to write a book regarding trans awareness, I have to admit that I was skeptical and uncertain as to what that book would sound like and/or look like. It's a big topic, and at some point in the not-so-long-ago past, her understanding and knowledge of this subject was new and unknown. This has since changed, and her interest, support, and awareness has grown and expanded, and now she has facilitated a collaboration in the form of this book: a helpful tool for those who are seeking some knowledge in the field of gender identities as a starting point or point of reference.

We simply don't know everything there is to know; that's just being honest with ourselves. Identifying when we don't know something is important; it can create an opportunity to shift the unknown to the more familiar. This is an ongoing cycle in all of our lives. Curiosity, compassion, and love have all led to this particular subject shifting from unfamiliar, unknown, and seemingly unrelatable to eye-opening and transformative.

This book was born from this kind of realization—the realization that people don't automatically have an understanding about different types of gender, gender expressions, and non-binary ways of life. It was conceived to invite people to explore their questions, curiosities, and understandings of gender; to help provide a platform to gain insights, connect people deeper with their own sense of gender, and create an open dialogue around gender as an experience rather than a label given at birth. It feels important to help facilitate conversations like these as there is no time like now.

Regarding my own transition, there is no real clear beginning, and I really don't see any clear end. I'm not sure if that's a trans thing as much as it seems to be a human thing. How do you know when you're done growing? Aren't we all forever evolving and learning how to be in the world? Aren't we all forever learning about who we really are? I feel like there is an unfolding process that happens in everyone's life that is unique to them. What this process looks like on the outside, or to the rest of the world, merely scratches the surface to the gates of our perceptions, inner worlds, and narratives of what we experience in our lives.

There is something that feels inherently difficult when it comes to writing about my transition. There are so many aspects and intricacies to the experience. It took me a long time to sit down and figure out how I wanted to contribute to this book. Transitioning is a long journey—so where to start? One of the first things that comes to mind is that anything that I have to share will be coming from my personal perspective and lived life. My voice could never speak to the "trans" experience in its entirety or to the trans population at large. No two lives are exactly the same, and no two transitions are either. Every transition is experienced differently with unique insights, dynamics, struggles, curiosities, goals, and so on. Even what it means to "transition" will differ from person to person—emotionally, socially, physically, medically, and more. My journey is my own. I am not the poster voice for the trans population.

The choices I have made in my life have been mine to make. This journey is not one that I could have planned out, researched to a point of full clarity, or fully understood before I began taking risks and chances to start acknowledging myself internally.

Being trans seemed to me like an impossible situation. The idea that someone could be born into the "wrong" body or gender just seemed… inaccurate, like life itself was playing a trick on me. I questioned the validity of my discomfort and curiosity for a long time before speaking about it and exploring it. Life often seems like a bit of a trickster—no?

As a disclaimer, I need to mention that I am first a human. What I look like now versus what I looked like ten years ago will be different to the average onlooker, or to those who didn't really know me, my eyes, my smile, or my inner realms. As I have grown as a person and transitioned further into a gender experience that feels more accurate, my exterior has echoed that experience. My smile is likely brighter and my clothes likely look more comfortable on me. I am certainly wearing them with more confidence. But who I am has not essentially changed. At my core, I am still me. I am also more comfortable, internally stronger, and have daily gratitude that I get to live as me. This seems like a gift. Daily activities that are necessary, like getting dressed, are no longer arduous, embarrassing, or confusing. Now, for the most part, I like the process of dressing and undressing.

I feel honoured that I have been able to explore my life in this way. It has been no small contributor to the unfolding of my life. The experiences of this have included the family I'm connected to, the friends I have now, those who have stuck by me through this process, my partner who has journeyed with me over many years, and the numerous people I have met along the way, sharing stories and experiences. Tears and laughter have been great healers—and so has courage.

The process of self-acceptance always takes courage. Finding yourself in the ebb and flow of life's learnings doesn't always feel clear, but this is life as we know it—trickery and all. I don't think I have met a soul who hasn't had moments of self-discovery, felt defeat, or shame, or who hasn't needed support along the way. I think we all need each other. Not one of us can figure it all out on our own. Being curious about each other's journey feels imperative at this point in time as we all face our inner worlds in the larger outer world that we are living in. If we identify that something about the concept of "other" creates discomfort, repulsion, or perhaps magnetism, doesn't that mean there is more to be known and explored?

As time goes on, I see gender increasingly as an intricate and creative aspect of human nature and expression. I feel less inclined to believe that gender has ever truly been only about male and female but rather is a broader spectrum of diversity in breadth and depth. As we all explore our balances of masculine and feminine, I think it's fair to say that these roles are in different balances at different times. I believe that our inner feminine and masculine aspects of self are in constant exchange. The exterior expression of that balance, which the rest of the world sees, is only a portion of the experience of self-expression.

Being trans has not been a detriment to my life, though at times it has for sure made somethings difficult, dangerous, and uncomfortable. I like to say it has created texture to my life. It has taken me into deep internal processes of searching for who I am and what life means to me. It has helped me develop a strong backbone and a keen sensitivity to intuition and safety. Overall, being trans has added character to my life. It has perhaps been an unconventional aspect of my personal story, but then again, every story is different.

I invite all who are interested to move beyond fear into self-curiosity, and to think about what gender means to you, personally. The more I have thought about gender, the more I recognize it as one aspect of self.

As a key aspect, it *has to* resonate with us as individuals so that we can live fully expressed lives—whatever this means to you. It's difficult to explain why exactly it doesn't make sense for me to live as a woman. I think explaining that would take a lot more time and words than are called for here. I *can* tell you, though, that if you are experiencing a deep questioning or curiosity around trying to figure out how to live as the gender you have been assigned at birth, and it doesn't seem to make sense, then it's worth questioning it and exploring this thread deeper and further. I would also encourage you to support and hold space for those who *are* in that headspace, even if you are not. Being supportive is something that, at its core, takes little to no effort. It's more about intention and being open and non-judgmental.

Thank you for taking the time to explore your understanding of gender, and for being open to those who are questioning and exploring their own. There are few things in life that feel absolute or straightforward. I think we can safely say that gender can be added to that list now as it has become more of a global conversation. We live in a vastly rich and diverse world full of uniqueness. Why box ourselves into thinking that people can only fit into two categories: male or female? The word "spectrum" has become a bit of a buzzword, and I say let it buzz around here!

Gender is a spectrum. We are all on it somewhere. Where do you feel you are?

Preface
by Suzanne Sherkin

I set out to write this book as the mother of a child who transitioned from female to male. I gave birth to a daughter, and I now have a trans son. Being part of my child's journey to find peace and health has been an extraordinary privilege that has left me wanting to share insights and learnings. I went through a kind of seven-phased emotional ride around Skyler's trans journey: first I was fearful, then defensive, protective, angry, curious, unconditionally supportive, and now publicly vocal. Each stage had its own roller-coaster ride of questions, concerns, and fears—all set against a backdrop of unconditional love and a singular hope for my child's health and happiness.

What I have come to understand is this: Being transgender[1] is no easy road. It is not a choice that anyone would make if they did not feel unequivocally, powerfully clear in their mind and heart that they had been born into a gender that does not match how they authentically feel.

The majority of us live comfortably in the gender to which we were born: male or female. If you have not felt the need to question your

....

1   According to Merriam-Webster, the definition of transgender is "of, relating to, or being a person whose gender identity differs from the sex the person had or was identified as having at birth."

gender, then welcome to the label of being cisgender[2]. I am raising my hand as identifying with this group.

Most of us in this category take for granted an ease of identity—that is to say, we don't deeply question our relationship to our gender. We accept that we are either male or female, and live our lives expressing our gender in our own style and in our own ways. This, however, is not the case for everyone. For a percentage of the population, the gender they were assigned at birth (i.e., the gender that appears on their birth certificate) does *not* match the gender they feel that authentically represents them. This book is about that population.

Transgender people are a marginalized community in society. It would be safe to say that's the case in most every country. Trans people can experience significant gaps in social and healthcare services for their particular needs, be victims of discrimination and harassment, face inequitable employment opportunities, high rates of suicide, and a host of other marginalizing dynamics. In some countries, being trans will even get you killed.[3]

On a more positive note, there are also communities, cities, and countries that provide significant support from families, schools,

....

2   Cisgender: "Cis" is a term from Latin meaning "this side of." Cisgender refers to people—the significant majority of the population—whose gender identified at birth (i.e., the gender on their birth certificate) matches the gender they identify with. People who are cisgender (often abbreviated to "cis") accept their birth gender as their authentic gender, and typically do not question their gender identity. The antonym of "cis" is "trans," from the Latin meaning "the other side of." People who are transgender (often abbreviated to "trans") feel a disconnection between the gender their were assigned at birth and the gender to which they identify. (See Chapter 7 for more definitions of words related to gender identities.)

3   The Human Rights Campaign reported that in 2019, 22 trans people were murdered in the US; Statista reported that in 2018, 125 trans people were murdered in Brazil, 51 in Mexico, 13 in Columbia; in Canada, Stats Canada does not record deaths specifically related to trans people, and keeps track only generally about hate crimes; in 2018, Stats Canada reported that 173 people were victims of hate crimes motivated by sexual orientation.

communities, and workplaces that champion gender diversity and create safe, supportive environments. In Canada, the federal government is becoming more progressive in this area of human diversity, and there are now laws in place to prevent gender-based harassment and discrimination.[4] Canadians have also recently seen the rules around passport information change, eliminating the requirement to identify as a specific gender. The implications of how this will play out internationally are still not known, but it's a great development towards "normalizing" gender diversity, both socially and legally.

I have also come to understand that gender questioning is a stage of curiosity—of searching for clarity about one's own relationship to one's gender. The goal here is to feel in sync with one's own body, and to feel authentically connected to the gender that defines us. Gender questioning can start at any age and can continue through one's lifetime. It can lead along many paths and result in many outcomes. No two trans people have the same experience or path in the expression of their transition—just as no two cis people have the same path in the expression of *their* living.

Each of us fits somewhere along the spectrum of gender identity. Perhaps you are a cisgender person who doesn't feel the need to question your relationship to your birth gender. Perhaps you feel like you fit in somewhere else on the spectrum between the binary points of male and female. Perhaps you feel more authentically connected to a gender that wasn't assigned to you at birth. Regardless of where you are on the range of gender identities, all of us fit somewhere on the spectrum. Gender diversity includes us all.

....

4   In 2017, the Canadian government passed Bill C-16 to help prevent violence and discrimination against individuals on the basis of their gender identity or their gender expression.

How we respond to each other regarding issues of gender can have a significant ripple effect. Impact—on individuals, families, communities, and workplaces. If you respond to difference with judgement, fear, or anger, the energy of that will impact the cultures around you. Respond with acceptance and respect, and *that* will be the tone of your impact.

My hope is that this book helps inspire your willingness to respond to difference with curiosity, openness, and support.

Knowledge, and having an open mind, is the only way to understanding. The more information and insight we have about how we identify with our gender, and how willing we are to allow others to express *their* gender, the freer and safer we can all be to live fully expressed lives.

Considerations in the writing

As I began to write, I discovered that the discussion about changing genders is very nuanced. How, for example, do you refer to the history of a trans person? Do you use their pre-transition name and pronoun for events pre-transition, or do you use their post-transition name and pronoun? It is not a straightforward answer. Some parents I interviewed for this book were adamant about using only the name and pronoun of their trans child's authentic identity, and never, ever used the name or pronoun pre-transition. "That person is gone…they just don't exist any longer," is what I often heard.

And what about family photos? Are all the pre-transition images removed, destroyed, and stricken from view and from memory? That's an interesting question. There is no single, simple or correct answer. I have spoken with families who have done a purge of all references to pre-transition—as requested by the trans family member. I have spoken to families who keep photos from all pre- and post-transition stages, use the "old" name[5] and pronouns when referring to past events, and the "new" name and pronoun when referring to current events. And I have spoken to families who keep all visual references to all the stages of the person's life and use only the post-transition name and pronoun to refer to them in both past and present events. It is this latter approach that my family has adopted.

In the interests of telling a clearly understood story, I am using my child's pre-transition name and pronoun to talk about life in a linear way. It feels strange now to use the name "Aviva" and refer to Skyler as "she," but the fact is, he spent the first twenty-one years of his life being referred to as female. That is a significant part of who he is now, and in my view, all of him needs to be valued as part of his growth and development as a fully expressed human being.

....

5   "Deadname" is the current terminology for a birth name that is no longer applicable or appropriate for use.

Introduction
from Dr. Helma

Dear reader, let me introduce myself. I am Dr. Helma Seidl, a registered social worker (RSW), psychotherapist, and I specialize in the subject of transgender (TG) and post-traumatic stress disorder (PTSD). I was invited by Suzanne Sherkin to assist and co-author this book on transgender identities. You're probably thinking, *Not another book on transgender studies; there are already so many.* And we thought so too. However, we worked very hard to make this book different from others.

In these pages, we discuss the experiences, thoughts, and fears that parents encounter when confronted with the reality of a loved one going through the challenges of being born in the wrong gender. The anecdotes of TG individuals provided will show you that the struggles you or your transgender loved one experience are shared by many. As a gender specialist, I have helped many transgender clients, parents, children, partners, friends, employers, and coworkers understand transgenderism. With my knowledge and understanding of this population, I have been privileged to help many throughout their journey. I hope that the transcription of this experience will continue to help and educate many others.

For my transgender readers, it is my hope that what you read in this book will provide comfort and will help you navigate the process from self-acceptance to finally finding your true self.

And for those wishing to learn more about transgenderism, I invite you to take this journey with us, and to view gender not as a binary in itself but rather as a *concept* that can encompass many different gender realities. I hope also that with this understanding of gender, your experiences with transgender people will be, in some ways, less overwhelming and even empowering.

Best wishes,
Dr. Seidl

CHAPTER 1

What does it mean to be transgender?

This chapter is written from Suzanne's perspective. Here, she tells the story of how her youngest child invited her into a conversation about personal identity and gender, and how that conversation significantly impacted the lives of everyone in the family.

TRANSGENDER

What does it mean to be transgender?

The night my youngest child, Aviva, approached me casually, life for the whole family changed. "Ma, can I show you some online stuff I've been watching?" It seemed an innocuous enough question. The two of us sat on the floor in our pajamas. I settled in comfortably, thinking that I was about to watch a cool new movie from her second-year university course. I was not prepared for what turned out to be an experience that would deeply change my family's life—and most significantly, the life of my child.

As I began to take in the content, I could feel my breathing slow to a near stop. What I was watching was story after story of young people in their early twenties—about the same age as Aviva—speaking about their gender like it was an intruder in their lives. They shared their intimate thoughts about how the gender they were called at birth did not match the gender they identified themselves to be. They spoke candidly about the incongruity they felt: the divide between what *is* and what they felt *should be*. Some talked about being born with a girl's body but feeling as though they should have been born a boy. Others spoke about being born in a boy's body and feeling they were really a girl. And there were those who felt most comfortable identifying in a fluid way, moving between male and female. Some spoke about the steps they had taken to bring their body image closer to what they believed to be their true gender identity and discussed the surgeries they had experienced. One person happily showed off their boyish-looking flat chest, making sure we particularly noted their still-fresh scars. Their chest looked so painful, but the look on their face was sheer elation.

Every video I watched was a raw, truth-telling expression of each person's journey to connect with their authentic gender identity. They all expressed their struggle to connect to the gender they knew themselves to be—and find peace along that journey. They were all on challenging and courageous paths. It took my breath away.

While watching these videos with my child, I felt a kind of delicate bonding occur between us—an intimacy that only comes from the sharing of truths with trusting hearts. My child was inviting me into a deep and private world. Putting aside the discomfort I felt in witnessing such new and initially strange ideas, I recognized that this was a moment of reckoning. I could feel Aviva watching me as I watched the computer screen. No matter how confused or uncomfortable I felt, I knew what was being asked of me: to embrace the moment, to be curious and non-judgmental, and to remain open-minded and open-hearted. The mere sharing of these videos with me was my child's invitation for unconditional love.

This experience took place in 2008. The world had not yet heard of Caitlyn Jenner or the television series *Transparent*. The public discussion about transgender rights had barely begun. Sure, I had seen movies like *Tootsie* (1982), *Mrs. Doubtfire* (1993), and *Boys Don't Cry* (1999), all of which involved stories about people with unconventional gender identities. But that was Hollywood, with its entertaining stories that were based on experiences far from my own life. This experience, in the moment, was so very close and very real.

Speaking personally, I had never given gender identification much thought before this night. I was born female. I was a girl. Not much to think about really. Like many kids, I struggled with figuring out how to fit in. Generally, we all have our rites of passage. My own issue was about stature: I was way taller than everyone else, and I struggled deeply with my awkwardness. I am humbly putting my own history into a new perspective: not fitting in because of height is one thing, not fitting in because of gender identity is quite another.

On that evening of learning, I recognized that I was being asked to imagine living in a body every day that felt foreign and unnatural. I was being asked to imagine that I could not relate to my own genitals, and that every day upon waking, I would wish that I were in a different body. These were chillingly uncomfortable thoughts—and yet, every single day, this was my child's experience. Before that night. I had no idea! I watched as Aviva gave voice to her authentic self and found the safety and freedom to emerge as Skyler. I witnessed a brilliant transformation from awkward to awesome, moving out of the darkness of discomfort into the light of renewal. I understand now that it was not a matter of "her" becoming a "him." *He* was already there. His identity was waiting to be discovered, to be tapped into and revealed.

Amy
(male to female)

Since public school, I knew that transitioning was something I wanted to do. I have always felt transgendered, even though I didn't know what it was. I put on a mask for so long. I trained myself to be as manly as possible – complete with bad posture and lowered voice. Now I have to undo all that and be conscious of my voice, posture.

Sandra
(male to female)

One of the most powerful moments I can recall was from early childhood – 5 or 6 years old. I remember waking up from a dream that felt so real in which I experienced a normal day, but I was female throughout the dream. I was utterly crushed when I woke up and realized that it wasn't reality. I had more of these moments growing up but this dream stands out as the most vivid of my own recognition.

For many of us, including myself, our gender identity is expressed without issue for the simple reason that we were born into a body that matches the gender we feel we are. If you were born with boy parts and you feel like a boy, then lucky you. The difficulty arises if you were born a boy but always felt like you should have been a girl—or born a girl and always thought of yourself as a boy. For those who are born into—or grew into—this gender discomfort, their search is to find a way to bridge the disconnection between their body and mind regarding their gender.

Many others have a different experience of their gender, which may include living with a duality in the privacy of their own world. "Eat. Pretend. Get by. Sleep. Repeat." might be a fair assessment of some people's relationship to their lives. Many will choose to make the decision to live openly in their authentic gender identity. That can mean taking steps to change their appearance as well as change how they engage socially.

Once Skyler stepped into his authentic male identity, everything in his life began to fit into place—and I mean *everything*. His art blossomed, he completed a post-graduate education program, he spent time with family. And most significantly, Skyler began to care about his own health, both mentally and physically. He sought out the medical support he needed and spoke openly with family about his issues. He was taking responsibility for his health and wellness in ways he had never done before. He was visibly happier. Skyler was still the same person as Aviva, of course, but it was clearly evident that he was now so much more comfortable in his skin. I was witnessing an astonishing shift that was impacting not only Skyler himself but our entire family dynamic. Aviva had been a withdrawn participant; Skyler was fully engaged.

Relationships are a reflection of how we show up for ourselves. When Skyler finally showed up *for* himself and *to* himself, every relationship in his life changed. This included his relationship to his older sister, Lauren. They had always been close—two sisters, just twenty-two months apart. But there were disconnects. Aviva just couldn't figure out the girl-like games that Lauren wanted her to be a part of, and Lauren couldn't quite understand the awkwardness of her sister.

Shopping for clothes when the two were young was always an interesting family experience. We would shop for Lauren in the girl's department and then head over to the boy's section. Aviva didn't want the colours or the cute styles of the girls' clothing. Instead, she preferred the rugged greys and blues of the boys'. So, with selections from both departments, the three of us would head over to the girls' change room and sort it all out. That pattern of shopping was such a habit for us that I had never attached any significance to it. It was only years later—and most recently—that those early family recollections are being remembered with a new perspective. So many indicators, both large and small, have now

Claire
(male to female)

A fairly common argument against transgender women made by critics and exclusionary feminists is that we don't deserve to be seen as women since we aren't treated as women and still live in place of male privilege. I understand that the feminist viewpoint seeks to point out how women are treated differently by men, and I agree that male privilege has marginalized women time and time again, but I think that it's unfair that trans women should be judged like this. We experience marginalization both as women and as trans women with overt discrimination – and all the while we're just trying to distance ourselves from our male pasts.

Sandra
(male to female)

My entire life has shifted direction since transitioning. I went from being shy, emotionally cut off, and unexpressive to being outgoing, personable, and open. I've heard from many people who have known me all my life tell me how much happier I now seem.

Claire
(male to female)

Affirmation is huge. When others acknowledge who you are and respect you by calling you by your new name or using correct pronouns, the effect is deep and profound. Humans crave love and attention from other humans. Affirmation is social love.

Jodie
(male to female)

Since fully transitioning, I don't wake up thinking about gender anymore. How cool is that?

occurred to me that spoke of Aviva's discomfort in her female gender. In those early years, I didn't know what questions to ask. I didn't know what signs to look for. I didn't know what I didn't know. None of us did.

After Skyler's transition began, his relationship with his father changed too. His dad, Hugh, had always seemed more comfortable with Lauren than with Aviva. He could sense Aviva's discomfort in her skin, as we all could, but it was never clear what the issue was, and he was never sure how to be around her. When Skyler shifted into his own gender comfort zone, his ability to be with others, including his father, changed too. Now there are no barriers, no unspoken curiosities about identity. The lines of communication opened more easily between the two of them, and that has continued to flourish.

What occurs to me as I review the unfolding history of Skyler's gender transition—and the beautiful authenticity it has allowed—is how essential it has been for him to have had a safe and loving place to reveal himself. With a family that supported him unconditionally, he was able to share his questioning and his concerns in an environment of unconditional love and acceptance. He could speak his truth to his family, and we embraced him for who he knew himself to be—not just for who we thought he was.

The research is very clear regarding the importance of family: a culture of love and support at home is a key contributor to well-being for trans youth as they address their gender questioning. The stats show that trans kids who are surrounded by support live happier, healthier lives both physically and psychologically, with less depression and fewer suicide attempts.[6] This makes sense, of course. For a person who feels the impacts of being part of a marginalized group, their family environment needs to be a refuge of safety, love, and unconditional acceptance.

Skyler's journey to live authentically has been fiercely focused. His clarity about wanting to live in his essential male gender has been inspiring. I have come to understand that it takes courage for a trans person to show up authentically. For a trans person, taking on a new name and a new pronoun is not just about a name and pronoun—it's about stepping out and being prepared to face whatever personal, social, or political obstacles may come their way.

Questions for personal consideration

» Do you feel that someone would feel comfortable and emotionally safe to speak openly to you about their gender identity?

- If no, would you be willing to develop this aspect of yourself?

6   "Impacts of Strong Parental Support for Trans Youth," Trans PULSE, October 2, 2012, http://transpulseproject.ca/wp-content/uploads/2012/10/Impacts-of-Strong-Parental-Support-for-Trans-Youth-vFINAL.pdf, PDF.

» If someone in your family revealed to you that they were questioning their gender identity, would you be curious and open to know more, or would you be fearful of their difference?

» Can you see yourself comfortably discussing your own relationship to your gender identity?

 – If yes, what stands out for you regarding how you feel about living as the gender that was assigned to you at birth?

 – If no, what do you think is creating a barrier to having this kind of conversation?

CHAPTER 2

What are some of the key ideas around gender?

In this chapter, you'll find a primer to understanding the key concepts of gender diversity. Four specific areas are discussed: the difference between sex and gender, gender identity, gender expression, and sexual orientation.

What are some of the key ideas around gender?

"Sex and gender binary are so engrained in us, we never really think about it, until someone comes along and makes you think about it."

—Emily Quinn, Intersex speaker and activist

It can be very confusing to sort through all the information and misinformation on the topic of gender. There are so many questions to consider. For example, what is the difference between gender and sex? What is the relationship between being trans and being gay or lesbian? What does being trans really mean anyway? Is a trans person someone who has had surgery? This chapter offers insight into the topics of sex, gender, transgender, and other associated subjects and terminology.

Sex and gender

The World Health Organization (WHO) clarifies that the term "sex" refers to "the biological and physiological characteristics that define men and women,"[7] whereas "gender" refers to "the socially constructed roles, behaviours, activities, and attributes that a given society considers

....

7   "Sex refers to the biological characteristics that define humans as female or male. While these sets of biological characteristics are not mutually exclusive given that there are individuals who possess both, they tend to differentiate humans as males and females." From "Defining Sexual Health," World Health Organization: Sexual and Reproductive Health, https://www.who.int/reproductivehealth/topics/sexual_health/sh_definitions/en/

appropriate for men and women"[8] This may sound pretty straightforward: sex is physical, and gender is behavioural. The reality is, however, these terms are definitely *not* that simple. Sex is not just about biology, and gender is not just about behaviour.

Sex

Generally speaking, we have been socially conditioned to recognize two options: male or female. These identifications are almost exclusively based on biology. If a person has breasts or appears to look female, we assume that they are female. If a person has a penis or they appear to be male, we assume that they are male. In short, someone's appearance or outward presentation is often how we determine their sex. These conclusions, however, are not always accurate. There are many factors that contribute to identifying someone's sex[9]; one's appearance does not always tell the whole story.

From a social perspective, most of us are stuck on needing to identify other people's sex. The question is, "Why?" One reason could be because of the way we're wired. Social scientists tell us that we instinctively respond to one another for one of three reasons:[10] survival (think food, and whether we're protecting our own food, or trying to get someone

....

8   "Gender, typically described in terms of masculinity and femininity, is a social construction that varies across different cultures and over time. There are a number of cultures, for example, in which greater gender diversity exists and sex and gender are not always neatly divided along binary lines such as male and female or homosexual and heterosexual." From "Gender and Genetics," World Health Organization: Genomic Research Centre, https://www.who.int/genomics/gender/en/index1.html

9   Biological sex is determined by many factors present at birth: the presence or absence of a Y chromosome, the type of gonads, the sex hormones, the internal genitalia, and the external genitalia.

10 Mark Bowden, *Tame the Primitive Brain: 28 Ways in 28 Days to Manage the most Impulsive Behaviors at Work* (Hoboken, NJ: John Wiley & Sons, 2013).

else's. Are we coming away from the encounter *as* lunch or *with* lunch?); mating (think sex or procreation, and whether we see this person as a potential sexual partner for the moment or the long-term); or social relationships (think friends, strength in numbers, support, and whether we need to protect ourselves in some way or if we can just share our personal resources freely). When we meet someone, our neurological and biological mechanisms get triggered in a fraction of a second so we can quickly categorize the person and know how to behave.

So, what does all this have to do with why we are so keen on identifying someone's sex? And why does it makes many of us uncomfortable when we can't easily identify someone's sex? Ultimately, we're wired to keep ourselves protected from uncertainties. Our wiring, operating primarily on unconscious levels, interprets uncertainties as possible danger, or a risk at the very least. Uncertainties make us feel uncomfortable, agitated, stressed, impatient, and a host of other things—and we behave accordingly. However, the more self-aware we are about what makes us uncomfortable and how this discomfort impacts our thinking, the

Pete / Joy
(gender fluid)

Gender was an issue for me early in my life. At 4, I went to the girl's washroom because it was easy. At 5, I knew I wasn't allowed to dress in a girlie costume at Hallowe'en. At 10, I explored the idea of wearing girl's clothes and cross-dressed only when I was in the house since I knew I had to keep this private and not tell anyone. At 17, I went to a clinic to figure out what was going on with me. In my 50s, Joy arrived. It was like having a religious experience. I could feel Joy take me over. It overwhelmed me. It was euphoric. It made me feel like I was Joy itself not just feeling joy. It seemed right to use Joy for my name.

Sandra
(male to female)

This is who I have always been so nothing really has changed. Transitioning is not an issue. It's not an event. It's not a problem. It's simply a shift in presentation.

Jodie
(male to female)

While my wife had known about my being trans for several years and had been supportive, it wasn't until I finally told her what I needed to do that began the chain of events that would forever change our relationship and our lives. Dressing occasionally as a female was one thing but living it full time was another. As expected, she didn't take it well. This began a very difficult time for all of us as my family worked hard to adjust to the reality of my new life. Throughout the ups and downs, my wife remained as supportive as she could and we continued to stay together as a family, despite her telling me that she will one day need to move on. Living with that knowledge has been the hardest part of my transition –knowing that the person I love isn't able to love "all aspects of me." I'm sure, though, it's as difficult for my wife since she is essentially now mourning the loss of her husband.

more in charge we are of choosing how we respond to different situations.

If it makes you uncomfortable when you encounter someone whose sex you can't readily identify, you're not alone. Many others feel the same way. The question, though, is "Why?" Why does it raise so many questions in us when we can't put someone in a category of male or female? It's an interesting question that has certainly created a lot of curiosity in my own thinking. In Chapter 9, I address these ideas in "Concluding Thoughts."

Determining sex by chromosomes

Chromosomes are part of the mix in identifying the sex of a person. Our cells contain 23 pairs of chromosomes that carry our genetic coding, among lots of other information. Of those 23 chromosomes, 22 are common to both sexes—only one pair carries the coding to develop our primary sex traits. Females typically have two of the same kind of sex chromosomes (XX); males typically have two different kinds (XY). This is where we get our generations-old thinking that biology defines sex. But biology is only part of the story, and it can get complicated. It is not uncommon, for example, for some males to be born with an extra X chromosome or for some females to be born with an extra Y chromosome. Sometimes, these additional chromosomes can create differences in body development.

Take a moment and imagine how you would feel if you discovered that your chromosomes identified you as a different gender than the one you had always felt you were. Perhaps test results indicated that you are a combination of genders. Would that scientific evidence make you feel different about yourself? Would it make you feel different about the gender you have come to identify with?

Determining sex by genitals

Genitals are the most common way we determine the sex of a person. We pretty much take for granted that a baby born with a vagina is a female, and a baby born with a penis is a male. But do genitals really determine sex? The answer is not straightforward.

Consider the small percentage of the world's population who are born intersex[11]—that is, they were born with ambiguous genitalia that includes both male and female traits. For example, a person might be born appearing to be female on the outside but having mostly male-typical anatomy on the inside. Or a person may be born with genitals that seem to be in-between the usual male and female types—for example, a girl may be born with a noticeably large clitoris, or lacking a vaginal opening, or a boy may be born with a notably small penis, or with a scrotum that is divided so that it has formed more like a labia.

....

11   According to InterACT, Advocates for Intersex Youth, about 1 in 1,500 to 2,000 babies are born with noticeably atypical genitalia; however, a lot more people than that are born with subtler forms of sex anatomy variations, some of which won't show up until later in life.

Jodie
(male to female)

Before getting out of bed each morning, I would often lay there thinking about being like the other girls and imagining what their daily routine would be as they got ready for their day. Opening my closet to get dressed for school and then work, I could feel my birth gender staring me in the face with a stern reminder that male pants and a shirt were my only options. As a comfort thing, I mustered the courage to start wearing female under-clothes as a way to feel closer to my true gender. Whether it was soft pretty underwear or a cami, it felt so good to be connected to my female self. Although risky, it made me feel closer to Jodie without anyone knowing.

Jesse
(parent of a trans son)

I saw the difference in my son after he came out as trans. It was like day and night.

There are also people born with a mosaic of genetics so that some of their cells have XX chromosomes and some have XY.[12]

The term "hermaphrodite"—which is no longer an acceptable label—was used historically to refer to people who have sexually ambiguous genitalia. The acceptable term now is "intersex." (See Chapter 7 for more on words and phrases.)

Determining sex by secondary sex characteristics

When we encounter someone, we tend to notice how they present themselves—their clothing, their overall appearance, their demeanor. If you don't live in a naturist society, then you will always be meeting people with their clothes on so won't be able to see their primary sex characteristics (i.e. whether they have a vagina or a penis).

We tend to notice people's secondary sex characteristics and consider them primary characteristics: facial features, body frame, voice, chest or breasts, and a myriad other overt and covert characteristics that give us clues for determining whether to categorize someone as "male" or "female."

12   InterACT, Advocates for Intersex Youth

Yet, these secondary sex characteristics do not necessarily provide accurate evidence to make that determination. What many of us tend to do—unconsciously for the most part—is make a judgement based on our expectations of what males or females look like. When the "signs" (or characteristics) are clear, we're comfortable; when they're not, we're uncomfortable. That discomfort can quickly escalate to negative reactions and protective or aggressive behaviour directed towards the person with unclear "signs."

The takeaway here is to recognize that people may not always be the sex we assume them to be. The question is this: Why does identifying a person's sex matter so much? Does someone's sex influence their values, personality, intelligence, capacity for empathy, or their ability to be kind or generous? Genitalia is a component of sex identification that says nothing about the actual person, and yet we remain endlessly curious about what is between someone's legs. The invitation here is to become a more conscious witness to your own behaviour. Does your behaviour change when you believe that you are speaking with a man versus when you are speaking with a woman? If so, how? Are you aware of the nuances of your body language, choice of words, actions, thoughts, and/ or your approach to engaging in the conversation?

Gender identity

"Gender" refers to our personal sense of gender—that is, how we perceive ourselves. If you identify with the genitals you were born with, then your gender identity is possibly more straightforward. If you were born with a vagina and were raised as a female, felt female, and never thought anything different, then likely your sex and gender are in sync.

This makes you a cisgender person,[13] and a part of the majority of the globe's population. If you find yourself feeling confused about why discussing the differences between sex and gender is even an issue, then that's another sign that you are likely cisgender. Generally speaking, gender feels "natural" for cis people. Those who question or struggle with the relationship between the sex they were born into and the gender they identify with most likely have a different gender story.

Fitting into male or female categories is not the full story of gender identity. Not everyone fits into this binary. Gender identity is a spectrum. One can feel gender-neutral, non-binary, agender, pangender, transgender, and more (see Chapter 7 for definitions). Gender identity can be all or none of a combination of these identities. It is a valuable reminder that these variations in gender identity have always existed through time, ancient cultures, and sub-cultures.

Today, we can have conversations that are backed by scientific research, and at least in some communities and countries, we can have conversations about the spectrum of gender identities that are accepted and supported within the political and social structures. Sadly, though, there are still many places in the world where these conversations cannot take place for political and/or social reasons. Whether it's a fear of change, a refusal to loosen the grip on old thinking, or just plain denial of anything outside of one's personal experience, there are many families, communities, cultures, religions, cities, and countries where open conversations about sex and gender is simply not allowed. Most of the world is staunchly attached to the concept of a gender binary that allows for *only* male or female identities with defined social and behavioural expectations for both.

....

13 "Cis" is a Latin word meaning "this side of," as in this side of the binary; it's the opposite of "trans" (see Chapter 6 for more definitions).

The takeaway here is that our sex—the biology that we are born with—does not always match our gender—i.e., the perception we have of ourselves. For those feeling this incongruity, there are choices: you can ignore the discomfort, or you can express it. Both have their perils.

Gender expression

Gender expression is how we express our gender selves to others and how it appears. Our gender expression comes across in how we dress, how we wear our hair, our gestures, mannerisms, and the sound of our voice. It's any aspect of ourselves that expresses how we want to be seen by the world. Gender expression can also include the name that we use to identify ourselves; this may or may not be the name given to us at birth. Our gender expression includes the pronouns we choose to be identified by—which may or may not be the pronoun that seems obvious to others. The more we deconstruct the ideas around gender, the more evident it becomes that "gender" is a socially constructed way of viewing and classifying one another.

The specifics of gender expression, particularly binary expression, are everywhere, and they begin from the moment of birth. Pink for girls, blue for boys—and so it goes on in endless ways of overt and covert influences: how we are raised, how we are spoken to by others, how we are marketed to, how we are remunerated for our work, how we are provided access to jobs … and on and on. Gender expression and the way people choose to live is not only a personal issue but a highly political one as well.

Sexual orientation

Our sexual orientation refers to the pattern of our romantic or sexual attraction. Our options for sexual orientation are varied. We could be attracted to the opposite sex (which makes us heterosexual); to the same sex (which makes us gay or lesbian); to both sexes (which makes us bisexual); to all sexes (which makes us pansexual); or we may have no sexual interest in any gender (which makes us asexual).

One of the key areas of misinformation in the discussion surrounding gender identity is how sexual orientation fits in. The key message here is that gender identity is different from sexual orientation. That means that your sexual and emotional attraction has nothing to do with your gender. For example, if you identify as a male (regardless of your genitals), you could be attracted to someone from a range of sexual orientations: another male; a female; a person who is trans; gender-neutral; non-binary; agender; pangender; genderqueer; or two-spirit). You could be attracted to all of these sexual expressions, some of them, or none of them. Who you are attracted to and how you express your own sexuality is completely separate from how you relate to your gender and how you express it.

Anywhere, anytime along the path of our lives, we can redefine our sex, our gender, and our sexual orientation. If we are in a politically and socially safe place to explore such thoughts, lucky us to have such freedom.

What it means to be transgender

To understand what being transgender is about, consider the following example. It is one of many possible gender narratives, with a reminder that no two gender transitions are the same regarding emotional processing or the stages of the transition itself.

Consider a baby identified as a boy at birth, raised as a boy, but who never related to being a boy and always felt more like a girl. He wanted to dress in girls' clothes, preferred to play with girls, and maybe even dreamed of being a girl. If this boy doesn't feel able to express these thoughts to his family or friends, he might need to keep his gender questioning a secret for many years, or maybe for his entire life. The older he gets, the more difficult it will be for him to keep his authentic gender identity a secret. If he feels safe enough in his environment to express his unconventional thoughts, he will likely want to outwardly identify himself in a female expression that feels more authentic. As a start, he might change his pronouns to "she/her," and change *her* name. She might choose to get surgery—top and/ or bottom surgery (see Chapter 5 for more on medical procedures) and might decide to take hormone replacement therapy to reduce her male features and enhance her female ones. With these outward changes, this trans woman may now feel that she is finally able to feel good about how she

Sandra
(male to female)

I felt a great deal of shame and fear around coming out and transitioning. The shame was about not being the person everyone expected me to be, while trying hard to portray myself as me. There was also shame around causing those close to me the stress of going through this with me. I felt fear over the "what ifs" that are associated with such a major change and that I was ultimately putting so much of my life at risk in an attempt to be a happier person–even though I couldn't be entirely certain that this transition would give me the peace and happiness I sought. It took a lot of work to overcome these feelings. Ultimately it boiled down to realizing that the other path–not transitioning–was worse and that the possibility of happiness was infinitely better than the certainty of despair.

Resa

(male to female)

This is who I am. It can't be wrong. Why can't I be accepted for who I am. I don't want to be judged by what's between my legs.

Sandra

(male to female)

I think that when people grieve for the gender they believed you to be, they have it wrong. They aren't grieving for you, they're grieving for the *idea* of you that they had built up over the course of your life. They grieve the loss of moments that they hoped to experience with you and the joys they'd hoped to share. I didn't have any of these things to grieve.

Giselle

(parent of a trans son)

We need to shift people from unconscious bias to conscious bias to unconditional acceptance.

is in the world—expressing herself in her authentic female gender identity.

Trans is about personal identity

Someone who identifies as transgender recognizes that their gender assigned at birth does not match the gender they identify with. Regardless of whether they have had any surgical procedures, take hormones, changed their name or pronouns, or changed their style of clothing, they are trans. This is a key point of understanding. They are trans even if they do nothing and keep their gender and identity private.

Every trans person has a different journey of coming to terms with the mismatch they feel between their biology and their identity. Every trans experience is a personal one with a journey that requires significant courage, determination, and resilience. Showing up authentically to one's family, friends, co-workers, neighbours, and community leaders is no easy road for anyone, particularly when that journey is outside the acceptable frame of reference.

As a family member, friend, co-worker, neighbour, or community leader, one of the best ways you can support a trans person's journey is to provide unconditional acceptance. Support can be provided in many ways. At its core, true support is about feeling, thinking, and behaving in ways that convey unconditional and non-judgmental acceptance for someone to step into their gender authenticity in ways that are most meaningful to them. Support can be as simple as holding space for someone to feel safe while listening with an open heart and non-judgmental mind.

A comment on pronouns

The use of pronouns has been one of the catalysts for public discussion and awareness of trans issues. The social construct of using gendered pronouns has long operated through the lens of binary identification: male or female. This construct is entrenched in the English language (and of course in many other languages). Traditionally in the English language, the singular reference to people has been "she" or "he." For more than one person, we have used "they."

With the increased public presence of gender diverse identities, the use of pronouns has developed into a public discussion—some would say debate. The pronoun "they" has been claimed by the trans and gender-nonconforming communities as a convenient way to address someone in a respectful way without needing to know their gender identity. Using "they" also ensures the person is not misgendered. This change in pronoun usage, however, seems to have created a lot of push-back from cisgender communities, with complaints that it contravenes their traditional grammatical usage (wherein "they" has been tradition-ally used as a plural reference). This new use of "they" has presented a change of language usage—and change, for many, is tough.

My own feeling is that language is a living entity. It needs to change, morph, and shift to reflect the current attitudes of the day. I recog-nize that not everyone agrees with this point of view. You may be a linguistic purist and see language as needing to protect from change, or you may be someone who embraces language as an every changing source of communication that is forever adapting to the cultural shifts of its users. Regardless of your philosophical viewpoint on linguistics, it is on each of us to ensure that we use the correct pronouns when addressing others.

A short guide to using pronouns

A male transitioning to female (MTF) is referred to as a trans woman, and she will likely want to be referred to with female pronouns (she/her). A female transitioning to male (FTM) is referred to as a trans man, and he will likely want to be referred to with male pronouns (he/him).

Here, though, is where it can get complicated. Not all trans people transition to a binary identity of male or female. Some trans people may see themselves as "genderfluid," meaning they do not identify exclusively with either male or female. Rather, these individuals see themselves as fitting somewhere on the gender spectrum between the binary points of male and female. For these people, the pronoun "they" is most appropriate as it encompasses both genders equally. If you are unsure of how someone wishes to be addressed, the best thing to do is to ask the person what their preferred pronouns are. If you are uncomfortable asking that question, simply refer to them by name. The invitation here is to be aware of your own language usage so as not to misgender anyone. Using the correct gender is a demonstration of respect and validation.

CHAPTER 3

Why are bathrooms such an issue?

Why indeed are bathrooms such an issue? This chapter is an overview of the current social narrative on the subject. It also includes personal stories about how gender issues play out in public bathrooms.

BATHROOMS

Why are bathrooms such an issue?

"When I was beginning my transition, I was hassled a lot when I used either the guy's or the girl's bathroom. If there wasn't a gender-neutral bathroom, I just had to hold my bladder and my bowels. It got really painful, and I started having medical problems because of it. I hesitated to go out on long outings so I wouldn't have to use public bathrooms. I eventually mapped out where the accessible single-stall bathrooms were so I could feel comfortable when I went out. This became an integrated part of how I navigated my life. To this day, I know where the best bathrooms are in different cities."

—Skyler Hagen

We live in a world that most often identifies gender in a binary way: male or female. This binary thinking influences just about everything: what washrooms we use, how and where we shop, the clothing we buy, the cars we drive, the movies we watch, the books we read, and on and on. Those in the business of studying and marketing social trends spend a lot of time and effort reinforcing our differences in a male-female construct. We're told that women buy more clothes than men, that women read more books than men, that women seek medical care more often than men. We see the reinforcement of these gendered roles and expectations in advertisements, movies, cartoons, and toys created for kids. The male-female binary permeates every aspect of our culture, overtly and covertly. Sometimes we take issue with it, but mostly we just absorb it—unconsciously.

Before my awareness of Skyler's transition journey, I never really paid much attention to the social politics of bathroom usage. Running in the background of my awareness were the news stories about trans rights in public bathrooms, and about whether the laws should favour bathroom choice according to one's biology (that is, their gender assigned at birth), or according to one's gender identity (that is, their gender they authentically feel). I heard the stories, but they didn't resonate with me. Those issues were not mine. They didn't affect me directly, so I mostly ignored them. That was then, this is now. It's always interesting to note how much more we pay attention to things when we have a personal connection to it.

What I have come to recognize is that being female has its privileges. Being male has its privileges. Being on the gender spectrum or transitioning from one gender to another complicates these privileges and creates compromised rights such as public-bathroom usage.

For many trans people, the bathroom issue is the biggie and represents the public battleground of being trans or gender nonconforming. Public bathrooms are generally where people in this marginalized community feel the least safe and the most outed. If a person presents clearly as falling into the binary—i.e., male or female—there is usually no issue. They walk into a bathroom that matches their gender expression, and no one takes notice. Trans people who are good at "passing"[14] generally don't get hassled, assaulted, intimidated, humiliated, or thrown

----

14 In the context of gender, "passing" refers to a trans person who presents themselves in a way that others perceive them as fitting into the expectations of male or female gender expressions (see Chapter 7 for more on definitions).

out as much as those who are viewed as identifiably trans or gender nonconforming.

Not passing as the gender you identify with can lead to violence, ridicule, inappropriate questions, or just plain rudeness. For those whose sex or gender expression does not match others in public bathrooms with binary male or female labels, the simple act of attending to bodily functions can be stressful and potentially even dangerous.

Aggression and violence in public washrooms were certainly a part of Skyler's experience. There was a period of many months, in the early stages of his transition, when it was not clear what his gender was. His facial features looked female, but with a short-cropped male haircut, he looked more androgynous. To others, it was unclear whether he was male or female. This midpoint in his transition turned out to be a difficult time for him.

In those early days, before his top surgery that medically altered his chest to look male, he had to bind his breasts. This meant using a wide elastic band to fit tightly around his breasts to flatten them. (It sounds painful, and according to him, it was.) Sometimes it was easy for him to go in and out of a public female washroom, and sometimes

Jodie
(male to female)

When I needed to answer the call of nature, I often had to stop and think about which restroom I was going to use. With my growing hair, people were starting to become confused about me so I would occasionally venture into the women's restroom when things were quiet, and that felt right. Most times though, I went into the men's room, which didn't feel right. Later on, men were doing double takes and appearing confused when they saw me in there, checking the sign outside a second time or simply walking out. While it was funny at times, it was becoming more uncomfortable as I began to fear for my safety. My gender confusion was never more prevalent than when using a restroom.

Skyler
(female to male)

In the early days of my transitioning, I was treated really badly by both men and women. I didn't look like I fit into one any gender so I was hassled a lot. I was beat up coming out of a public men's bathroom and yelled at in a public woman's bathroom. I got so paranoid about using public washrooms that I just didn't like going out in public at all. I got really good at holding my bladder and my bowels but it wasn't a good thing. I ended up with a lot of pain—emotionally and physically—with lots of headaches and backaches. Even to this day, I find public washrooms difficult to navigate. Men's washrooms can be dangerous places for a trans man.

it wasn't. He has a *lot* more stories than he has been willing to share with me about his public washroom experiences, but I do know that for the first few years of his transition he was harassed, yelled at, and physically pushed out of female washrooms. Men's washrooms were potentially more dangerous. He has experiences of being threatened, beaten up, and followed outside to be hassled. So much for feeling safe in public washrooms.

The bathroom debate has been raging publicly in the US and to a lesser degree in Canada since the 2010s. As trans rights became more publicly debated, more reports were published of people protecting their rights—on both sides of the debate divide. The issue came down to one question: should people choose a public bathroom (including locker rooms and change rooms) based on their gender identity, or based on their gender assigned at birth?

On the one hand, there is an expressed fear that sexual predators (i.e., men pretending to be trans women) would suddenly have access to female washrooms where they could harm women and children. On the other side of the rights debate are those fighting to have the freedom to use public facilities that matched their gender identity.

The issue heated up around 2016. In the US, a bathroom bill was passed that required trans people to use the bathroom that corresponded with the sex on their birth certificate. In Canada in 2016, headlines were of a more civil nature. Teens called the fight to restrict washroom access "ridiculous" and "absurd."[15] CBC News talked to students across the country to hear their thoughts on the "bathroom debate" and heard many conclusive arguments stating, "I don't understand why this is an issue. We just want a place to go pee." You certainly can't argue with that reasoning!

Clearly, concepts of privacy and safety carry different layers of meaning for everyone. Add to that the nuances of cultural behaviours and expectations and you have a stew of controversy about the boundaries of gender in the name of privacy and safety.

In 2017, legislation was passed in Canada (Bill C-16) that added gender expression and gender identity as protected grounds to the Canadian Human Rights Act and the Criminal Code.[16] Those opposed to this loosening of restrictions around washroom usage eventually quieted down when research began to be published showing that there was no relationship between the non-gender-identified facilities and rates of crime in public washrooms.[17]

. . . .

15   CBC News, posted May 24, 2016

16   The law adds gender expression and gender identity as protected grounds to the Canadian Human Rights Act, and also to the Criminal Code provisions dealing with hate propaganda, incitement to genocide, and aggravating factors in sentencing.

17   A study conducted by the UCLA School of Law followed crimes in washrooms in major cities for two years and found no difference in crime rates between cities that had adopted transgender policies and those that had not.

The new reality is that the boundaries of gender are shifting in seismic ways. We are no longer a society where our gender identification can be neatly ticked off in one of two boxes: male or female. We are now in a world where people are openly expressing a spectrum of gender identities and moving fluidly within the broad range of possibilities. How these identities are expressed differs from person to person, and accessibility to public bathrooms needs to reflect and embrace this broad spectrum of gender expression. Everyone needs to be assured that public spaces, including washrooms, are safe for everyone. No one should be made to feel different, unwelcome, or shamed for being who they are.

It is very good news indeed that gender neutral bathrooms are becoming more commonplace. They are now found on college and university campuses, in public schools, and in many restaurants and shopping malls. It has been long in coming and slow to catch on—locally, nationally, and globally. We need to celebrate the small shifts taking place towards making public bathrooms safe places for the full spectrum of gender diversities.

CHAPTER 4

Reflections: A Transition Through Genders

By Skyler Hagen

This chapter provides a first-hand narrative of lived experiences from someone transitioning from female to male. As Skyler walks through different social and interpersonal elements of this transition, he asks readers to share his questioning about gender "norms," authentic self-expressions, and social constructs.

TRANSITION

Reflections: A Transition Through Genders

What I am sharing is a collection of memories and insights into some of the internal processes that have gone into my transition over the years. As I mentioned in the Foreword, no two transitions are the same. Self-acceptance as well as discovering and uncovering myself have been wonderful gifts of these combined experiences. I celebrate my decisions to transition, and I can say that with certainty.

As someone who has transitioned from female to male, I now walk in the world as a man—a white man. I believe this is important to note, as the narrative I share is one that is deeply affected by my access to white-male privilege. While exploring gender awareness, it is important to also consider the intersecting dynamics of race, ethnicity, and culture, especially because xenophobia is so present in the world today.

Consider how the ripple effects of oppression are affecting the global community of humanity in overt and subtle ways, and have done so throughout history. It is not hard to see, even with the limited statistical data that exists, that there are disproportionate barriers and higher rates of gender-based and racialized violence towards members of the Queer Trans Black Indigenous and People of Colour (QTBIPOC) population. This needs to change.

Our decisions profoundly impact the world around us, whether or not we are conscious of these impacts. It matters deeply how we engage with and reinforce or resist social constructs, wherever we meet them. We need to be talking about the presence of racism and prejudice; we all have a responsibility to engage this reality and shift it. Consider that staying silent and/or complicit in discriminatory patterns reinforces those same messages of discrimination. How we engage those around us, as well as how we choose to approach life is part of a rich and powerful dynamic full of opportunities to inform and manifest the world in which we want to live.

...

The chapter below explores some of the internal processes that have occurred within me related to my transition. We all make choices that radiate out into the world. This narrative is about some of the choices I have made and the insights and rippling effects that I have experienced.

Walking Through the Unknowns of Transitioning

I first came out as gay in my late teens. It was something that I had a sense about for a long time, though I never acted on it because I was happily dating men and it wasn't something that concerned me very much. (I would later come to understand that I am queer rather than gay or straight, as gender doesn't seem to matter as much to me as who the person is themselves.) When the opportunity presented itself to explore the world of dating women, I remember feeling both elated and terrified. Waves of internalized homophobia washed over me as I recalled my first intimate encounters. This was a torturous and lonely experience.

I remember cycling through those memories riddled with anxiety, unable to sleep or rest all night, feeling like I had done something disgusting and wrong. I felt completely messed up that I felt this way in the first place. What was going on? How could I be so accepting of others and totally phobic at the same time? Dualistic thinking is flawed. Rarely are situations cut and dry.

I had gay friends and had always known gay people. Somehow though, when it came to *me* being gay, I struggled with my own internal processes and judgments. Years went by, and as I dated women and found my fluidity and confidence in this part of my life, I began to better understand myself as a young adult. There was a large, visibly queer population where I lived, and I had made friends with people who accepted me for who I was, regardless of how I identified. In my life so far, I have 'come out' twice—once as gay and once as trans.

Through reflection and self-exploration, I think I was aware that I was a 'boy' when I was in early grade school but gender didn't mean anything to me at the time, so I just kept on living my life. When I turned ten, I realized that I wasn't magically going to become a boy, and so I decided to become a girl. It seemed like that was my only option. The first thing I did was grow out my hair. I had always had short hair and though I liked the way it looked and felt, it seemed like most girls had long hair, so, I decided to make that statement for myself and others to see. I tried to forget about feeling internally different for another ten years.

"I never thought I was a girl. I actually never thought I was any gender. I was called a girl when I was growing up but I didn't really connect to any gender. I was just me. I started questioning my gender when I was about 10, and when my breasts grew, I knew I had to be a girl. It was weird. As my body grew, I felt more and more uncomfortable in it. When my breasts grew, I hated them. My mom offered to have them made smaller but I just wanted them removed. I didn't even like to be naked alone."

"If I had heard at age 5 that I could be any gender, it would have been an easier road."

The summer before I went to university I hitchhiked around Canada and part of my trip was to find out what it meant to be a "woman." I met all kinds of women, young and elderly, strong and eccentric, kind and daring. It was an incredible few months. I connected with a deep respect for women, but I realized for the first time—consciously—that I wasn't one. I remember feeling disheartened, confused, and totally uncertain about what that all meant for me in my life.

Shortly after I went to university, I met an openly trans person for the first time, and it blew my mind. I remember feeling in awe. It occurred to me that they must feel a sense of relief because they had "figured it out," and I wondered if they felt as lucky as I perceived them to be. My mind fixated.

I started remembering things about myself and the things I had pushed away for years. It was an intimidating and anxiety-provoking subject to explore. The more I read about transness in my gender-studies classes, and spoke to people about gender, the more I realized that I wasn't going to be able to "forget" this part of my life again. This was a very painful period. It wasn't at all clear how I was going to do anything about it. The concept and choice was so big. How could anyone be that certain in themselves to make such a big decision? And what did "making a decision" actually mean? How did people transition?

I remember struggling with the fact that I could read about other people's gender experiences and trans narratives and it felt like they were writing about my life. How did they know? I hadn't told anyone.

I eventually started talking to select friends about what I was feeling and thinking about. At the time, I lived in a house with seven other people. One day, I drew a line on a piece of paper with the words "girl" written on one side and "boy" written on the other. In the centre, I wrote "neutral." I asked some of my closer housemates and friends to mark on the line where they thought I was. I was curious about how they perceived me. It was hard to know what was in my mind, and I didn't know what others' experience of me was. I felt I needed to bring the conversation outside of myself.

This was not a gender test. It was a way for me to start a dialogue with others about this incredibly pressurized subject that I couldn't stop rolling around in my mind. I wanted to slowly bring others into my internal dialogue and get a sense of how I was perceived. What I experienced was really interesting. It created a dialogue I didn't know I was able to engage in. Each person I asked had an interesting reaction. Not a single person put me at one end or the other, not even those who weren't quite sure what I was even asking. Most people saw me close to the neutral mark. It varied which side people perceived me as being closer to; some people put me slightly left of neutral towards the girl side, or slightly right towards the boy side. I remember feeling an unbelievable sense of relief that not one person told me that they thought I was a girl. Everyone had somehow picked up on what I was internally questioning. It was a significant moment for me and gave me a lot to think about.

It's interesting to think of gender as a concept. We all have both masculine and feminine aspects of self that weave through us, regardless of the gender we identify with. I suspect that many people who don't identify as trans or question their gender might hear a variety of responses if they asked their close friends to clarify where they perceived them to be on the line of girl—neutral—boy.

I spent the next couple of years spinning thoughts and trying to understand myself regarding gender. I remember typing the word "transitioning" into YouTube and later more specifically "transitioning FTM" (female to male). What popped up would become one of the most helpful tools in my journey. I saw videos of people from across the globe posting entries about their gender experiences, and about the stages of their transitions.

I remember that I went through a roller coaster of emotions and visceral experiences when I was watching those videos. Seeing that so many people were also on gender journeys so to speak had a really calming effect on me. Recognizing that I wasn't alone was deeply validating. People were transitioning in "real time," and it wasn't just an entry in a book. I could watch their documented processes. I also remember feeling physically nauseous when it came to watching surgery results and watching people doing hormone injections on the screen. It was a real wake-up call to me that if I decided to pursue a medical transition, it was likely going to be a long road ahead. It felt overwhelming and did, in fact, take years to wrap my mind around before taking action. It was hugely comforting, though, to know that so many people were in this together.

I spent time reclusively in my room fixated on figuring this thing out—and that created its own set of problems with my university housemates. It was voiced to me that some people felt I wasn't participating

"I didn't know that transitioning was an option until I was about 21 when I discovered the documentary, "Just call me Malcolm" and other videos I found on YouTube. Hearing other people share their stories and concerns really helped me understand my own journey."

"Since my transition, I'm so much more capable of connecting to my emotions because now I'm finally comfortable in myself. Now, I can easily connect to who I am and express how I feel."

"Transitioning has been a huge undertaking but an amazing process. I'm glad I did it gradually."

enough in the house, that I wasn't taking enough of a part in house activities. It was hurtful to hear this, and yet I wasn't able to express my feelings about my confused state of being. I was struggling on a regular basis to face the world outside of my room. Simply going to the kitchen for food or water created deep anxiety. What if I ran into someone and had to speak with them? I had days and weeks of experiencing this internal blasting of anxiety.

I was intimidated by people of all genders. I felt trapped in my body, embarrassed about my physicality, and at the height of feeling alienated in myself and from others. I was struggling with both my self-confidence and mental health. It was a difficult time.

It takes a lot of energy to constantly be examining and exploring personal consequences and possible outcomes of choosing to transition—regardless of how supportive people are around you. These decisions are not small. They don't inherently need to be torturous or completely depressive, but the weight of such dynamics is very real. There are so many things that must be taken into consideration, like social and cultural structures and pressures, political or religious restrictions, personal risks to losing life—or, at least, losing life as one once knew it. There is no clear path when it comes to transitioning, and no certainty about how a transition will "turn out."

There are so many questions and finite details that one thinks about when approaching a transition. "If I admit to myself that I'm trans, what does that mean for me in my life?" "What will my life look like?" "What will it mean for others around me?" "How will people relate to me?" "Will I have to change my name?" "How do I choose a name?" "How do I go about changing my personal documents so that my I.D. matches me now?" "What pronouns am I comfortable with?" "How will I dress? "Will I be able to afford to buy new clothes to explore this?" "What will this mean for me at work?" "How can I expect others to understand if I'm not sure that I'm completely comfortable with it myself—yet."

Then there is thinking about relationships and love, and the possible outcomes of what this may mean for current and future partnerships. Will I be accepted? Will I be desirable to others? Will these desires go past being fetishized? "Who will love me? Will I be lovable?" "Who will be attracted to someone like me?"

The questions can seem endless at times. It can be incredibly daunting when looking up from the base of such a mountain of unknowns. There is no one way to "be" as a trans person. I don't think there is *one way* to be as a person in general. Everyone must figure out what feels best for them and take it one day at a time. This process can be energizing as well as difficult. For me, it felt like I was experiencing a continuous roller coaster of emotions.

...

I was always a big-chested person. I say "chest" because using the word "breasts" has always felt embarrassing when referring to myself. It was difficult for me to look like I was flat chested. I often wore over-sized clothing and longed for cooler weather so I could layer clothes and hide my curves strategically. It had been obvious to me for many years, even before I decided to transition, that my chest was a physical and emotional source of anxiety and stress.

I remember talking with my mom about getting a chest reduction in high school. I was an athlete and my back often hurt from the weight. Back then, I was trying to find ways to be comfortable in myself without connecting the dots to gender. I was told by the doctors that a reduction could be done to look "natural" and in proportion to my body.

I decided not to pursue this surgery. I had wanted a smaller chest than what I was told was possible at the time.

Instead of a reduction, I eventually began binding. Binding means using materials to press your chest to your torso to flatten the lumps with pressure. This can be a painful situation. Because my chest was so big, I had to wear a lot of binding layers. In doing so, I gave up being able to breathe easily, endured chest and back pains, and strained my skin with the non-breathable pressure. I did this for years. This eventually became unsustainable.

One day, I booked a consultation with a plastic surgeon who I had heard of on YouTube, offering "top surgery." I was lucky that my infinitely supportive sister came with me to this consultation. It was a surreal experience. I had to take off my shirt for this stranger who then talked about what he could do with the chest I had, and told me how he could create a closer version of the chest I was looking for. At the end of my consultation, I spoke to the woman who was in charge of booking surgeries and dealing with payment. It was an incredibly expensive procedure, but they had an opening in a month. For the first time, this physical change could become a reality. I left sweaty, nervous, excited, and totally scared.

I didn't reach out to that clinic for another year. It took me that long to process the idea that I could actually shed my body of what turned out to be ten pounds attached to my torso. I needed to emotionally process the possibility of transformation and ask myself the zillions of questions over and over again. I needed to be one hundred percent certain that I wasn't going to want, at any point in my life, to carry a baby to term and then breast feed. I thought of many more scenarios, ones that I wanted to make sure I was comfortable with before making this decision. It is a huge decision. I wondered how I was going to afford it. I wondered how my family was going to react.

I eventually decided that with or without support from anyone other than my sister, this was something I needed to do. I was at a point where I was preparing emotionally to be rejected from my family and knew that I would still hold strong to myself. That was how solid I was in my decision. "If I'm going to live my life, I want to be able to live as who I feel I am. If my family can't accept that, I am not going to shy away from my truth just to make them feel better about themselves."

Though I was emotionally and physically intimidated as well as frightened, I felt I had reached a point of clarity and courage. I didn't want to live in a world where I had to turn a blind eye to my inner knowings of self. I came to realize that in this life I need to trust myself, my intuition, and my volition. No one can live a life for you. If you know who you are and what your needs are, it's imperative to create that life for yourself. This for me was a decision many years in the making. I felt certain that, at some point, I would need to make a decision. Years of processing were all combining

Curiosity is human nature. It is important, however, to respect people's choices without needing to know for yourself what their life is about. What is it about needing to know what is beneath someone's clothing that is so intriguing to people?

It's interesting to think of gender as a concept. We all have both masculine and feminine aspects of self that weave through us, regardless of the gender we identify with.

into a moment of action in the now. I picked up the phone, called the clinic, and booked my top surgery. Done!

As my transition unfolded, my family did come around. It created an opportunity for my father and I to get closer, and that relationship developed into a new and beautiful connection. My transition seemed to be a catalyst for us to connect in a way that we had not found before. Our relationship continues to strengthen to this day. It was one of the aspects of my transition that was totally unexpected and happily welcomed.

The relationship with my sister also strengthened. It seemed to solidify our connection to a much more fluid friendship. She has always been completely supportive, even when she didn't understand what I was going through. Now, in the dynamic of sister and brother, we flow with so much more ease than ever before.

The relationship with my mother also become closer. We have always had a really strong, loving, and supportive connection, and as it was with my sister, we flowed with more ease and transparency. It feels like through my transition I got to know my family more, and they certainly got to know me—the authentic me.

I feel absolutely lucky that this has been my experience. I certainly didn't know that years later this would be my story. While approaching my transition and going through internal turmoil, I didn't know such a positive outcome would be possible—*could* be possible.

I recognize that this is not everyone's story. In fact, it's very common for people to have the opposite experience of mine. I am not saying that my family all came together magically because I decided to transition. I think in becoming more authentic in myself, I felt I had nothing left to really lose and my family all met me in that place. I can't emphasize enough the positive impact that supportive and safe friends, family, and community have played in my life. I know this too is not everyone's story.

Unexpected Lessons of Learning to be Male

It is amazing how strong the structuring of gender 'is' or has become. As a trans person I have found myself in the throes of day-to-day interactions of many kinds, feeling like I need to present 'male enough' to allow or create smooth interactions. What I mean by smooth is uneventful—not bringing attention to the fact that I am not what people think I am. This dynamic is interesting, because ostensibly, in those moments, I am encouraging social norms without trying. In the process of not drawing attention to myself, I am also unintentionally facilitating the silencing, on some levels, of gender expression. This may be to support my physical or emotional safety. It also speaks to the fact that I sometimes want to fly under the radar and be stealth (see Chapter 7 for a definition). To just be me as I am feels like a basic human right. I'm Skyler. I don't introduce myself as, "Hi, I'm trans Skyler."

In queer circles, I have found remnants of this as well. I have felt many times that I am not visibly 'queer enough' or 'trans presenting enough,' because at this point in time, I pass as male. I often feel I am overlooked, erased, and quickly dismissed from queer spaces in general as I look very much like a "dude." The messaging then becomes that I am an outsider and am not really a part of what's going on. As someone who used to be very visibly queer, I find this part of my transition to be really interesting. I have never been one to identify fully with one group or another, but the shifting through social dynamics and circles has changed many times for me so far in my life. What a concept it is to be accepted in one chapter of my life and dismissed in the next from the same crowd of people.

There are many people who accept all genders and gender expressions, and there are also many people who carry misogynistic or misandry views of trans populations. Trans narratives need to be navigated in all kinds of ways with all types of populations. Queer identity or not, challenging cis-normativity is something that the trans and non-binary populations are constantly dealing with. Unfortunately, there is a lot of gender shaming in communities. There is also a great deal of acceptance.

The impact of my transition goes beyond me. My partner for instance, an amazing queer woman, has also experienced somewhat of a shift in her sense of queer identity. When we walk down the street, we now look like a "straight" couple. It wasn't always this way, but it is now. It's our own little secret that we sometimes smirk about in public spaces, whispering things to one another like "if they only knew!" We may look straight, but we are not. This goes for queer and non-queer spaces.

We often talk about how this has impacted us, checking in with one another about this sense of both gain and loss, felt simultaneously. My own transition journey has never been about trying to pass as

"I've gone from a straight girl to a gay girl and now appear as a heterosexual guy. I've taken on many forms of gender identity and have been with a large spectrum of genders. Authenticity comes down to the person—not the gender."

"Before I transitioned, I thought I was going to be unlovable. Now I feel very worthy of love because I can love myself. Maybe the world is ready for more than two genders.

If you could be you, why not be you? What girls are and what boys are amounts to broken social norms. Our global community is all changing."

straight. When the two of us enter queer spaces, we are often read us as straight. At the beginning of my transition, it didn't occur to me that my actions would have such an impact on my partner's identity. We met after I started transitioning, but I was gender fluid and we "read," then, as being a queer couple. Decisions we make can have a significant ripple effect.

I recognize the lines between perception and reality often blur, and I respect the fact that, to the general population, I look like a cis man. I accept that I now feel less welcome in some spaces where I used to feel at home. That's unfortunate and all part of my learning journey. I do think, however, that all spaces, including all queer spaces, need to feel safe for those seeking refuge, support, and community. No one said any of this was going to be straightforward. We are all figuring it out as we go.

Another aspect of my transition that I had to learn was a new public role in relationship to women. I notice now that sometimes at night when I walk down the street, a woman will cross to the other side. I soon realized that they were crossing because they considered me a male and therefore possibly dangerous. I actually remember feeling that way myself, pre-transition. Being aware of this, I have since adjusted the way I move in the world, and now at night or in dim lighting, I cross the street when I see a woman walking so as not to make her feel anxious in any way. One of my new regular lines of internal questioning is to ask myself if I am creating any unintended impacts in the spaces I am taking up. I am constantly readjusting my thinking *and* acting to reflect a respectful male gender role.

Learning "how to be male" has been full of life lessons about human behaviour and gender dynamics socially, politically, historically, and more. It has been one of the most natural things I have ever done, and also one of the most difficult. It has also been a humbling experience, requiring me to re-examine myself throughout all the stages of my transition. For this, I am genuinely grateful.

Humanness and Trans Visibility

I feel drawn to continuously connect to a feeling of being balanced by acknowledging the spectrum of gender within myself, regardless of my exterior presentation. I have stopped being concerned about any pressure to "pass" or to present as visible "enough." Instead. I embrace the intricate myriad expressions and experiences that feel most authentic to me. I feel like I am in an ongoing process of finding my style, as well as my most honest and expansive version of self.

People often share that they are surprised when I tell them that I'm trans. This is a whole other aspect of considerations in my life now. "Should I tell this new friend or colleague that I'm trans?" If so, "why?" If so, "when?" As a mental-health counsellor, I also need to ask myself when and why it feels appropriate to share this aspect of my life with clients. Some clients ask about my gender identity for the sake of their own comfort, and if I have lived experiences of queerness or gender fluidity. I feel other clients may lose respect for me or stop sharing about parts of *their* lives if they were to find out about my life. The process and decisions to engage in self-disclosure extends beyond the borders of social and professional realms. This is now my day-to-day life. There will never be a single day in my life that I am not trans. That is just part of who I am. There are fewer and fewer days where it feels like work to be aware of this. My transness is part of the lens that I see the world through. I cannot separate that from myself, and to be honest, I wouldn't want to.

There are times when being outwardly trans feels radical and progressive. I often wonder if this gets erased when I ease back into the

There is no one way to "be" as a trans person. I don't think there is one way to be as a person in general.

Though I was emotionally and physically intimidated as well as frightened, I felt I had reached a point of clarity and courage. I didn't want to live in a world where I had to turn a blind eye to my inner knowings of self.

comfort of "passing," or simply walking down the street with access to white male privilege. Sometimes I feel like I am undercover, and at other times I feel like a fraud. Days like these come and go.

Trans people are not all visible. Your neighbour or co-worker may be trans, and you may never know it. On the other hand, you may be very aware of it. The way each trans person outwardly manifests themselves is different. Sometimes this is an intentional choice and sometimes this is the reality of a transition. I often wonder, for people who are not trans, how it registers to witness a visibly trans person, or to know that an individual is trans regardless of what stage of transition they are in—whether they "pass" or not.

Is it difficult to see the person as their presenting gender if you can sense a stage of 'in between?' Do these thoughts continue even if a known trans person "passes?' Is it hard to withhold judgment or voyeuristic tendencies to be extra curious about them? Do you wonder about aspects of people's lives that you wouldn't otherwise think twice about if they weren't trans such as, "How do they have sex?" "What did they look like before?" "What are they 'trying' to look like?" Do you wonder what they have done about their genitals?

Curiosity is human nature. It is important however to respect people's choices without needing to know for yourself what their life is about. What is it about needing to know what is beneath someone's clothing that is so intriguing to people?

I pose this as a question, because as a trans person, I am asked questions about my body all the time, and not by people who are hoping to pursue me as a love interest. This is not an uncommon thing to experience as a trans person. It can be really off-putting and anxiety provoking when people who have nothing to do with my sex life ask me about what's in my pants. Why this aspect of my transition should mean something or anything to them is beyond me. I have never approached anyone and asked them about their genitals, or about their naked body beneath their clothing. What is between peoples' legs is their own business; it is not for publication. It is a natural thing to be curious. What we do with that curiosity, however, really matters.

Bodies are interesting things, aren't they? We all have our hang ups about our physicality about one thing or another. Comparing ourselves to one another though doesn't often end well for us mentally. It really depends on the day, and what we're hung up on. For me, some days, it can still be hard to look in a mirror and see a trans body. Some days, I love what I see, and sometimes I find my scars attractive and courageous, even sexy.

When I look in the mirror and see my hair thinning, I wonder, "Should I stop taking testosterone?" I consider that "a man my age should ... have a thicker beard," or if I were a cis guy, I would have had...." These are figments of projections as there really aren't specific ways any gender presents across the board. Off days come and go. I often remind myself to let go of the seriousness of life and find humour where I can. Humour definitely adds levity and acceptance in spades.

On some level, we all notice subtle and some not so subtle changes as the years pass and our bodies get kissed with the marks of time, making memories and continuing to experience life has this effect on our physical bodies. It's a trade-off for our youth. It's life. For the most part, I am really happy with my body and the outcome of my transition. I have no doubts in my mind that I made the right decisions.

We all face big changes and decisions in our lives. The subjects and details differ greatly. When it comes to gender, there can be many questions and a lot of opportunity for true self-expression. The thing is, we all have many differences, as well as similarities. I say embrace them all and don't limit yourself or others along the way. Live your truth.

CHAPTER 5

Transgender, transitions, and the social and family environment

By Dr. Helma Seidl, PhD, MSW, RSW, Psychotherapist

Typically, a trans person, their partners, and their family members each have questions about navigating the challenges of understanding gender dysphoria, the transition, and the fitting-in process. This chapter is organized into four sections, addressing questions and concerns that are commonly heard from parents, spouses/partners, and children who have a transgender parent. The chapter also seeks to answer questions from trans people such as what to do when people don't understand their gender dysphoria or their need to transition.

ENVIRONMENTS

Transgender, transition, and their social and family environments
By Dr. Helma Seidl, PhD, MSW, RSW, Psychotherapist

Both transgenderism[18] and homosexuality were part of my early extended-family experience, and I soon became aware of the psychological, physical, social, and environmental impact that transgenderism can have on an individual and their family members. I also recognized the effect it has on their social and work lives. My early experiences also fueled a passion for conducting research to better understand whether gender is fixed (binary male or female) or fluid (needing both male and female). Ultimately, my experiences and academic pursuits developed into a career as clinical counsellor and doctor in social work, where transgender individuals represent eighty percent of my clientele, from six to seventy-five.

This chapter is organized into four sections, with each section addressing questions I commonly hear from parents, spouses/partners, and children who have a transgender parent. I also address questions from trans people seeking answers of their own.

....

18   Transgenderism: This term is considered by some sources as being controversial, however it is still currently in use in transgender literature.

» **Section 1—"My child told me that they are trans."**

The first section addresses some of the questions and fears parents have when their child expresses gender dysphoria and wishes to live in the gender identity they know is the right one for them.

» **Section 2—"My mother/father told me that s/he is transitioning or that s/he is cross gender."**

The second section addresses questions commonly asked by children who have a transgender or cross gender parent.

» **Section 3—"My spouse/partner told me that s/he needs to transition."**

The third section deals with questions that someone may have when a spouse/partner transitions. Many questions often arise regarding their relationship and the raising of their children.

» **Section 4—"Am I transgender—fixed or fluid?"**

The fourth section is directed at the person questioning their own gender identity. Common questions regard when to come out, and how to help others understand their own need to transition.

There are many questions often asked by those involved in the life of a transgender or cross gender[19] individual, including parents, family, friends, and co-workers. To avoid repetition to the extent possible, some questions will be addressed in one section, only, even though they might fit into other sections.

After reading this chapter, please remember that many more questions will likely arise. It is my hope that all your questions about gender diversity and gender expression will open doors to positive dialogue,

....

19   Cross gender: This term, used under the umbrella of transgender, refers to people who identify as both male and female, and who feel comfortable with a gender identity that shifts between both genders.

expanded knowledge, an opening of minds, and ultimately, greater acceptance of gender diversity amongst loved ones and others in your community.

Following is a guide to the many acronyms and words you will find throughout this chapter and likely in other literature:

CG = Cross gender

Dysphoria = Despair

FTM = Female to Male transgender

GD = Gender Dysphoria

HRT = Hormone Replacement Therapy

MTF = Male to Female transgender

OHIP = Ontario Health Insurance Plan

QOL = Quality of Life

SRS = Sex-Reassignment Surgery

TG = Transgender

TRT = Testosterone Replacement Therapy

Section 1–Questions and concerns of a parent whose child is questioning their gender

This section addresses common questions and fears voiced by parents with a child who has expressed GD and who wishes to be acknowledged as, and live in, the gender identity they believe is the right one for them. When the trans person is a teenager, they often hear comments such as, "When did you know?" or" I never saw it coming," or in the case of male to female transition, "You always *were* such a boy."

Several factors can influence the age in which a child may begin to hide their "real self," compared to what parents or other family members might remember. Societal influences play a large role in all our lives, whereas parental influences or peer pressure may play a role in only part of our lives. Regardless, each factor can have an impact on the coming-out process, on understanding where one "fits in" and on the overall mental health of the gender dysphoric (GD) child.

My clinical experience, as well as my research, suggests that many more FTMs appear to question their gender incongruency at an earlier age than do MTFs. Burnham's (1999), Seidl (2008). The question now is, "Why is this the case?" The answer might be that the behaviour of little children can simply be cute. A three- or four-year-old boy (MTF) putting on a ballerina outfit while dancing and singing is entertaining. However, after age five, society expects this same child to now behave like a more typical boy.

A little girl (FTM) can behave as a typical "tomboy" without societal pressure until puberty when more typical "girlie" behaviours are expected. Parents may enjoy showing off their children, but ultimately, they too wish to meet expectations of family, friends, and their community by having their child "fit in." The difference is that it is not unusual for an eight-year-old boy who wants to wear a dress or dance to be labelled a "sissy," even by family. Whereas, a tomboy girl, perhaps working with her daddy in the garage or playing hockey, can be a pride and joy. That is, until a certain age.

Unfortunately, these social perceptions can negatively impact the social-emotional wellbeing of children and their development of trust, due to their need to hide their "true self." These perceptions also play a role in the severity that GD has on the individual's mental health.

With this said, we need to make sure that we do not assume that all tomboys are masculine women or transgender. There is nothing wrong with a masculine female just as there is nothing wrong with a FTM. Ultimately, it's about diversity and acceptance.

Currently, there is a greater awareness of transgender than there has been in the past decade, with information and personal stories available on the Internet and discussed in the media. So, it is not unusual for parents and their child to come to their medical professional declaring, "I am ready for hormones, and I want them yesterday not tomorrow!" A common question asked by family members is, "At what age should a child be given a diagnosis of GD?" From my clinical work with GD, I would advise families of a young child not to seek a definitive diagnosis but rather to work with the child to enable him or her to express their feelings and the gender behaviour they feel is appropriate for them.

Help your child explore gender diversity. Consider speaking with daycare staff or others involved in your child's care to ensure that he or she doesn't experience bullying because of their gender expression. Let the boys paint their nails, play in the kitchen or with dolls, and let the girls play sports or pretend to be fire fighters. The key is to let children explore and grow up feeling comfortable around gender. This approach will help both adults and children learn acceptance of diversity. Letting a child grow up

"I would advise families of a young child to work with the child to enable him or her to express their feelings and the gender behaviour they feel is appropriate for them rather than seeking a definitive diagnosis at an early age."

"The key is to let children explore and to grow up feeling neutral about gender. This approach will help adults and children alike to learn acceptance of diversity."

in an open-minded and diversity-accepting environment will increase trust and self-confidence, while a lack of acceptance of diversity will affect mental health and might lead to depression or anxiety, to name only a few issues.

Often a parent's main fear is of their child being a victim of bullying. Parents can be strong advocates for children by speaking with teachers and with other parents to deal swiftly with both nuanced and overt bullying. In some cases, parents may need to go beyond getting angry or pointing fingers, and change schools for a child with GD. The main goal is to find ways to be an ally to your child. We know that your child will benefit psychologically from your unconditional support, and that the bond developed from this support will be one that can never be broken. Remember, above all, it is love and support that matters to your child.

Parent's often ask, "How concerned should I be about this phase?" and "Will my child switch back?"

At a young age, children form their identity and their own expression of gender, and we need to support the child to be flexible and true to themselves. Parents often ask how they know if their child is going through "a phase" or a genuine gender-identity questioning. The truth is, we don't know. The child knows, and we need to be patient and support the child during their critical developmental stages. It is understood that children form identities and expressions of gender at a very young age, and that parents can support their child in allowing them to be flexible with their gender and true to themselves. A child is likely to be themselves and express gender differently at critical developmental stages. When professionals talk about this topic, we often use the words "desist" or "insist" in the context of true GD in children. "Desist" implies forbearance or restraint as a motive for stopping or ceasing, as in desist from further efforts to persuade. In contrast to this, "insist" means to maintain (definitions by Merriam-Webster). If it is a developmental phase, it desists (stops); if it is "true GD" it will continue. Sometimes it stops for some time due to peer pressure, but it will come back at a later point.

Parents may struggle with knowing how to explain how or why their child persists in behaving as a different gender than is apparent. Parents, imagine that you are walking with your child in a stroller down the street and someone stops to ask, "Is it a boy or a girl?" You could answer, "I don't know. My baby hasn't told me their gender yet." Not surprisingly that individual may walk away with a bewildered look on their face. Consider also having to explain to your child that she/he was not invited to a birthday party because their friends and parents did not understand his/her gender identity.

Indeed, both parents and their children usually want to fit in to their social community without negative attention. For this reason, many parents might push to get their child diagnosed with GD and start on hormones so that it is easier to say to others, "My child is a boy" or "My child is a girl." Additionally, many parents want a clear and identifiable gender in the face of cultural challenges from ethnic, religious, or other background considerations. As well, some parents may just need everything to fit into an uncomplicated little box, but this is not always what life experiences provide.

Fortunately, there are many great books presenting relatable stories of diversity for children at all ages. Consider: *My Princess Boy* (Cheryl Kilodavis; Illustrated by Suzanne DeSimone); *The Boy with Pink Hair* (Perez Hilton; Illustrated by Jen Hill); *It's Okay to Be Different* (Todd Parr); and *10,000 Dresses* (Marcus Ewert; Illustrations by Rex Ray), to name a few.

If transition is needed, when should it be started?

When a decision has been reached that a transition is needed, it is time for medical expertise. Decisions about the stage of physical development will need to be considered before beginning hormone intervention. It is recommended to start hormone blockers before puberty or when secondary sex characteristics become obvious. For males, intervention often begins before they show body or facial hair, or their voice begins to change. For females, blockers are recommended before menstruation or breast development. These amongst other physical changes, when different from one's true identity, can cause many transgender people great internal dysphoria.

Internal dysphoria is not visible to the eye, and many individuals start early to hide visible signs of gender not compatible with their true self. In the case of FTM, many may start binding their chest, cutting their hair short, or wearing male or androgynous clothing to avoid appearing physically female. Throughout the years of my clinical practice with transgender people, FTM clients have often appeared younger than their true age. They have been assumed to be a young boy, given that their voices had not yet changed. Having the ability to "pass" as male or appear externally as their true gender can help young people in the transition process. However, for these same FTM individuals, the female body can present as more feminine as they reach their thirties, and then result in a more severe GD than previously experienced.

Another set of challenges present themselves for MTF youth. GD can be more difficult at an earlier age for MTF when facial hair begins or when the voice starts deepening. It may be the case that these individuals quickly appear more masculine in their overall body development and size, making it even more difficult to appear female. Additionally, finding clothing or footwear can complicate the efforts to "pass."

In addition to visible signs of puberty, the transgender youth at this time also becomes acutely aware of peer pressure and their need to "fit in." It is at this point that many youths appear to "give in" to peer pressure or attempt to "pass" as gender conforming to avoid attention or being bullied—emotionally or physically. Other youth might start to repress their true selves, internalize negative attitudes, or withdraw from friends or family. Not surprisingly, it is when exhibiting these behaviours that many transgender youth show signs of anxiety, depression, obsessive compulsive disorder (OCD), or other challenging mental health conditions. With suicide rates in teenagers already higher than other populations, the addition of managing the complications of the transgender experience has been recognized to increase feelings of despondency and suicidal thoughts.

Puberty is a critical time for parents to talk about mental health issues, especially if there is a family history of these issues. If depression or anxiety runs in family history, it is important to know. In the transition process, we only address depression or anxiety related to GD, and these issues are generally resolved after transition. However, if there is a genetic component to depression, anxiety, or other mental-health issues, the treatment such as psychotherapy or medication needs to continue even after the transition process is completed.

In the adult transgender population, there are other considerations that can adversely affect mental health. These considerations can include financial stability, family support, and social and work contentment.

A common question asked is, "How many people are transgender"?

This question is often asked by parents, family members, peers, colleagues, and the transgender person themselves. Usually, this question is related to a fear of being alone in their experience, or of being an outsider.

Generally, we look at research to address this question, reviewing numbers and percentages of the number of people in the population of interest. However, there are many factors that come into play when addressing this question, such as what the purpose and accuracy of the research is, and who is paying for the research, since they can influence the outcome. Also, research results can differ depending on how researchers ask questions, and who is included in these studies. Since gender is on a continuum, some people might not feel included or think they don't fit into this category. The fact that many people are not "out" makes it beyond challenging to gain access to transgender people and determine the size of the population.

In my clinical practice, as well in my own research, I have learned that many transgender clients will have in the past avoided anyone or anything that might identify them as transgender to others, preferring instead to stay hidden at all costs. Others may not have had Internet services, or other modes of access to being included in studies or otherwise being "counted."

"It is understood that children form identities and expressions of gender at a very young age and that parents can support their child in being flexible with gender. A child is likely to be themselves and express gender differently at critical developmental stages. This self-expression depends on how much support they get and how safe they feel."

"When a transgender parent is ready to come out to everyone, the most important thing to keep in mind is that children should be told. Asking children or others to keep a secret can negatively affect mental health for everyone involved."

Research findings can help minimize stigma and shame, or simply validate the transgender experience for both individuals and for society-at-large. Gaining access to funding for additional research often relies on statistical accuracy regarding the population. Clinicians, including myself, are continually asked to provide statistics, where no others exist about our practice with this population.

Often researchers will include only participants in certain "groups" or those within a population who are very outspoken, or even advocates. Statistics, therefore, are very specific and can miss including those who find themselves on the continuum of gender diversity. Others who may not be included in research may be those who identify as CG or gender fluid, or those who have not yet accepted their GD, or believe their dysphoria to be mild and thus not severe enough to be included in studies. These, and other factors, contribute to providing an incomplete or inaccurate picture of the transgender population.

Sex-reassignment surgery (SRS)[20] is often used to create statistics. Yet these statistics fail to include the many who may want to have SRS but are not able to afford it. Currently, SRS can be covered or funded by some provincial health plans but not by others.

We know that more MTF SRSs have taken place primarily because this surgery is often less expensive, by two-thirds, than a typical FTM surgery. Adding to the complexity of counting SRSs to achieve an understanding of "how many people are transgender?" is that a typical MTF transition will include a one-hour surgery (approximately). Whereas, a typical FTM transition can include top surgery to remove breasts, a hysterectomy, and for some but not all, bottom surgery. Each

....

20 The term "sex reassignment surgery" (SRS) refers to medical surgery for people presenting with gender dysphoria. "Gender affirming surgery" (GAS) and "gender confirming surgery" (GCS) are currently popular terms that tend to be used in social, non-medical contexts.

of these procedures can require many hours in surgery. Bottom surgery generally includes up to three separate surgeries. As well, there are different types of surgeries such as phalloplasty or metadoioplasty, and people might see different doctors for the different types of surgeries. Unfortunately, all these scenarios can make it difficult to accurately understand how many people may be transgender.

To be funded for an SRS in the province of Ontario, for example, the Ministry of Health and the Ontario Health Insurance (OHIP) require a medical diagnosis of GD, one year on hormones, and one year of full-time living in the true gender self. Most surgeons will require two letters of recommendation, which have to be written by a medical doctor, psychologist, doctor of social work, or a master of psychology or social work. For an FTM, a hysterectomy must be completed before bottom surgery. For an FTM to have a chest reconstruction or hysterectomy covered by OHIP, there needs to be a written referral by a medical doctor or an endocrinologist. Not unlike those in the general population requiring knee, heart, or other surgeries, there is a requirement for a medical diagnosis for OHIP to fund the procedure. I am aware, however, that some transgender individuals feel that gender specialists should not be involved, given that this is an informed-consent decision process.

When we talk about TG care, we often differ between the medical diagnostic model and an alternative model. The *Informed Consent Model* is the alternative model that allows TG clients to access HRT or SRS without undergoing mental health evaluation and an assessment letter from a mental health/gender specialist. However, many endocrinologists or gender surgeons will not start HRT or perform SRS without letters from a gender specialist.

Throughout history, SRS has been performed around the world. A few well-known cases include Sophia Hedwig, born Herman Karl, who underwent MTF SRS in 1882 Germany, and Lili Elbe, another MTF, who underwent SRS in 1933 (Fausto-Sterling, 2000). Often described in historical accounts (see Devor, 1997) is the case of an English FTM, Michael (Laura) Dillon, who underwent SRS in 1949.

Of interest, it was the development of anesthesia during World War I and II, and the experience of treating war injuries, that allowed surgeons to work on the ambiguous genitalia of Intersex (IS) people and to attempt penile reconstruction. Until 1952, it appears that SRS was performed quietly, without the knowledge of the greater public. This changed when an American, George Jorgensen, went to Denmark to have a highly publicized SRS and returned as a female named Christine. There is now a growing body of literature on the history of sexuality, gender, and transgenderism available to transgender individuals, families, peers, and their healthcare professionals.

Drs Pierre Brassard and Yvon Menard, plastic surgeons from Montreal, operate Canada's only sex-reassignment (SRS) clinic. In an interview with *Le Journal de Montreal* (Nov. 13, 2001), these doctors stated that fifteen percent of their clientele came from Canada, and that they had performed 230 vaginoplasties for MTF patients. Of note, there is a significant difference between the numbers of surgical procedures performed in 2001 compared to the number performed in 2018 (see Table 1 below). This Canadian clinic has highly regarded surgeons and staff, and they are recognized for their quality of care. Some of my clients, who also became patients of this Montreal clinic, consistently reported how respected and safe they felt in the care of this team.

"Effectivement; les Drs Brassard et Menard effectuent quelque 230 vaginoplasties (transformation d'un corps d'homme en corps de femme) par année et une dizaine de phalloplasties (transformation d'un corps de femme en corps d'homme) (In fact, Drs Brassard and Menard perform about 230 vaginoplasties in 2001 (*Le Journal de Montreal*, Nov. 13, 2001).

Data for Sex Reassignment Surgery (SRS) and other gender related procedures from 2013-2018

Table 1

Procedure	Assignment	2013	2014	2015	2016	2017	2018
Genital Surgeries	M to F	241	245	247	309	376	470
Genital Surgeries	F to M	38	27	55	45	51	48
* Other Surgeries		206	240	293	295	453	394
Total		**485**	**512**	**595**	**649**	**880**	**912**

*Other surgeries include, but are not limited to, mastectomies, urethral construction following phalloplasty, penile implant insertion or testicular implants, and other minor corrections. (GRS Montreal, Dr. Brassard March 21, 2018)

Another reason for the controversial findings about the ratio between MTF and FTM might be that MTF often created a greater cultural shock and their presence frequently dominated and still dominates the written historical as well as medical cases, which further supported the once-prevalent belief by Hirschfeld (1910) and Pomery (1975) that transgenderism was an exclusively MTF phenomenon. Pomery (1975), an expert in the field of sexology, reported in his first writings that the ratio of MTF to FTM was 50 to 1, and over the years he changed his assumed ratio to 15 to 1, and soon after he found that the ratio of MTFs to FTMs was 4 to 1 (Pomery, 1975).

Gender clinics and specialists in the field still disagree when it comes to the ratio between MTFs to FTMs. Green (1998) found that FTMs were in the shadow of MTFs for a long time but that they are now coming forward in large numbers. This supports newer reports of more equity in the ratio of MTF to FTM clients. Brown and Rounsley (1996) reported that, in the previous five years, the MTF to FTM clients in their clinical care fluctuated from as high as 20 to 1 at times, to 3 to 1 at others. Eighty percent of my clientele in my private practice are transgender. There has been an increase in FTM clients over the past eight to ten years, which brings the ratio of FTM and MTF clients to 50-50, which likely reflects as equal numbers of MTF and FTM coming forward to request assistance.

Other considerations
Employment or getting promotions after transition

Another issue to consider is the matter of gender inequality at work, particularly regarding promotions, and how ideas are recognized or respected. The difference between males and females, clearly still an issue in the general population, is also an issue seen in the MTF transgender population. The new issue of gender inequality for an MTF can severely affect quality of life after transition. If an individual has a stable job and active social life, then problems with mental health are often minimized.

Parents often ask, "Did I do something wrong in raising my child?" Try not to place blame on yourself. It is important to support your transgender child by educating yourself, getting support, and understanding that diversity is a natural part of life in every context. In fact, it is now understood that nature has created the material basis for diversity and that sexual orientation and transgender behaviour are evident in primates, marine mammals, fish, hoofed mammals, carnivores, marsupials, rodents, and insectivores, as well as in humans. (Bagemihl, 2000)

Male-to-male and female-to-female attraction and transgender behaviour in animals are not new discoveries; some of the earliest testimonies of these phenomena date back to ancient Greece. Gender variability in mammals is also reported by Aboriginal populations around the world; their belief in this observable fact is well-documented in anthropological research. In 1895, Zoological research on this subject was conducted by Alexandre Laboulmene (Bagemihl, 1999). From that time onward, the scientific study of animal homosexuality and transgenderism emerged, found recognition, expanded, and in the twentieth century, there was an increase in literature with more than 600 articles on the topic published by the scientific community (Bagemihl, 1999).

Expectations of gender roles are learned, and they influence our beliefs and values. These learned beliefs can lead to popular myths and misconceptions, which can ultimately have an enormous impact on transgender identity development and quality of life pre-, during, and for some, even post-transitioning.

Section 2–Questions and concerns from children whose parent may be trans or cross gender

The age of the child will determine how open we can be, and what the transgender or CG parent should say. We often see that if the child is still young and other individuals around them, such as the non-transitioning parent and grandparents, are supportive and are allies for the TG/CG parent, then the child will also be accepting of the transitioning parent.

Coming out is as important to the TG individual as is being honest to the children. If children are older, however, we can also deal with opinions or attitudes of friends, their parents, teachers, and principals. Typical occasions, such as the children's friends visiting, can create stress for the transgender person or the children, producing shame, guilt, secrets, and great tension in the home environment. The TG person may be home relaxing in their true gender form and the young person might say, "My friend is coming over and does not know about you. Please don't embarrass me. Please change your clothes."

It is not uncommon for trans people to change their new name several times in the beginning of the transition process while they find their identity in the way of self-expression and social gender expression. However, to be ready to come out to their child/ren, the transgender person first needs to self-accept and have established their identity and their new name by which they want to be addressed. This will help to not add confusion to the family and child/ren.

If the TG individual switches back and forth between names and pronouns, we often hear family members making statements such as: "Are you sure? You don't seem to know what you want."

The most important thing is for the parent to tell children only when the TG person is ready to come out to everyone. Asking children or others to keep a secret can negatively affect mental health, for everyone involved. A TG individual knows well how difficult it is to keep a secret and how this affects mental well-being. Others should not be expected to keep this information secret.

A common question is, "What name should the child use for the TG parent?" Children often fear losing that parent, so if the mother transitions, FTM, and they already have a father, don't expect them to call you dad. The same holds for MTF, if they already have a mother, and may not want to call you mom. When considering what name the child should use with a TG parent, it is best to sit together and ask the child what name they are comfortable with. It could be a nickname, such as shortening Dad to "D." Language is powerful. Words and pronouns come with social expectations. If you agree that they call you Dad, but you are MTF, then do not become frustrated if in public you are referred to as Dad and you get weird looks.

Family, friends, co-workers, and the transgender person are each struggling with language use, especially with pronouns

How we address a person, especially regarding the pronouns we use, reflects how we relate to an individual. How we address someone, such as with she/he, father/mother, the way we speak with the individual, and the pronouns we use when speaking about others and our own life can create confusion. Language usage can create external and internal conflict for everyone involved.

Language has great power that can be used in positive or negative ways. Gender diversities are also found in linguistic structures. Our everyday discourse on gender shows the influence that the social construct regarding the gender binary has on transgender individuals. Pronoun usage can be a very important, and potentially anxiety-inducing, component of the transition process. Language is learned, and with this, we learn social constructs of gender and socially accepted and expected behaviours.

Examples of these social constructs can be found as far back as the year 621 BC (and even earlier). These constructs illustrate the self-acceptance of transgender individuals as well as their social acceptance or non-acceptance. Additionally, language is constantly changing. The word hermaphrodite, now outdated, is an example of changing terminology; the current term is Intersex. Other examples of changing terminology include the diagnosis of "gender identity disorder" to "gender dysphoria," "transsexual" to "transgender or trans," "he/she" to "them," to name a few. (See Chapter 7 for more definitions.)

The number of genders used in different languages and the addition of new words into dictionaries are important subjects for the transgender and CG individual, especially in different age groups. For example, the word *queer* is now commonly used and accepted in the younger population, whereas this word can be insulting in older populations. It cannot be overstressed how important it is to ask the transgender person how they want to be addressed, as well as how they identify themselves (female, male, transgender, trans, CG or other).

There are 6,800 known languages spoken in the 191 countries of the world. Of these, 2,261 have writing systems. To find a complete list go to http://www.yourdictionary.com/languages.html. Likely there are even more languages now since some dialects in many countries are now considered a language. Within linguistic structures, "gender" is not always considered as a binary construct. The number of genders in different languages varies from two to more than twenty; some are referred to grammatically and some referred to as lived genders (*The American Heritage Dictionaries*).

The English, Latin, and German languages each recognize three types of gender variations: masculine, feminine, and neutral. A gender-neutral or gender-inclusive pronoun is a pronoun that does not associate a gender with the individual being discussed.

The gender of certain nouns that might be neutral in the English language can be either masculine or feminine in other languages. The pronoun "parents" in modern English is neutral in terms of gender. For male or female, in French and Spanish, there are two variations used reflecting either masculine or feminine. In the Scandinavian and Dutch languages, there are four variations used: masculine, feminine, neutral, and the common.

The common variation is a gender-like distinction. However, there can be a variance in the use of this pronoun. The common variation is also found in the Algonquian language of Aboriginal peoples of North America. These gender variations correlate, in part, with animate and inanimate objects, one referring to people, animals, and spirits, the other to things (*The Columbia Encyclopaedia*).

Why do we talk about language in such detail? It is my hope that this discussion can help family, friends, co-workers, and even the transgender individual understand their struggle with acceptance. In my clinical experience, it is often helpful to change pronouns using a neutral pronoun before using the gender specific one in the transition process.

In the context of language, we also can and should address androgyny and intersex. Since it is such an enormous genetic/medical subject, the condition of intersex, needs its own chapter or even book. For parents of an intersex child, my suggestion is to seek help from a professional medical or a gender specialist to better understand your child and to make the right decision for them. Do not be afraid to wait. A child can be given a neutral name, used for either gender. Also make use of neutral colours rather than typical pink and blue, and try to be flexible and open with toys.

There are many different opinions of the source of the German, English, and French languages. One opinion is that the English language is said to be a hybrid of Latin and Germanic languages, as well as influenced by French. Whereas French, Spanish, Italian, Catalan, Romanian, and Portuguese are all descended from the Latin of the Roman Empire.

The term "gender" dates back to the fourteenth century, and the etymological meaning comes from the English *gendre*, the French *genre*, and the Latin *genus*, generic. "Androgyny" is a term even older than gender. Its meaning was derived from the Greek *androgynos*, from *aner*, *andros* a man + *gyne* woman. It was also used as a synonym for hermaphrodites—individuals born with both male and female sex organs, or those who possess both male and female characteristics. The term we use now is intersex.

In 1974, Sandra L. Bem published her measurement on androgyny called the *Bem–Sex Role Inventory*, which is still in use. Previously, androgyny was often viewed as a passing phase in gender choice and was often not included in the spectrum of gender diversity. Androgyny is often found in adolescents when they are establishing their identity and self-expression. Now, androgyny is an accepted and a used term found in the greater continuum on the gender spectrum.

Not everyone wants to be boxed into the gender binary and therefore they may opt

"The important thing is for people to recognize what they need, to take their time, and to not be forced to conform to fitting into the gender binary of male or female."

"While some people do not want to be diagnosed or labelled, a diagnosis is required, at this time, in order to acquire funding from an insurance body."

"What's beneath one's clothing is no one's business but their own. Regardless of one's decisions or procedures, they are still in their true-gender self–fixed (female or male) or fluid (both)."

for androgyny. This term provides individuals with the possibility of expressing both masculine and feminine genders. Androgyny is often used in the context of gender fluidity, in adolescents, the transitioning TG individual, and the CG individual. For some people, this might be a developmental phase, and for others, a natural persistent stage.

In gender transition, an individual's androgynous stage is clearly an emotional-physical-sex developmental stage of gender-identity development and expression. In the early stages of the transition process, there is a time when the phenotype—the physical characteristics or specific traits determined by both genetic make-up and environmental influences of a transgender individual on hormones—is not clearly identifiable as male or female. Gender passing at this stage is, for some, often difficult since the individual is not clearly identifiable as feminine or masculine.

Ultimately, use of language is important not only for the transitioning individual or the CG individual, but also for family, friends, and other peers (e.g., at work and in the community). Language use often causes many internal as well as external problems. Language can lead to confusion but also give the transgender and CG individual reaffirmation on passing and integration into their society.

In language, there is constant change; new words are continually being added or taken away. In my years of working with this population, I have learned many new terms for people on the spectrum of gender. There are too many terms to include them all, and every generation has new ones. It is, therefore, of utmost importance to ask the individual how they want to be addressed.

Another question often heard is "What do I say?" when children ask a transitioning parent, "Am I transgender too?"

Answering this type of question depends on the age of the children. As a clinician, I often ask the young children, "How do you feel?" I reassure them that it's okay to be themselves. When children have questions, parents should talk with them. With older children who have a TG parent, we look at their level of maturity and openness to talk.

If children are old enough to understand the concept of genetics, parents can talk about TG running in families, and that you, as their parent, might not be the only one in the family history to be transgender. If there is another TG individual in the family, talk about this but also let the child know that not everyone in the family is TG and that the most important thing to keep in mind is to be themselves.

Section 3-Questions and concerns about a spouse or partner who needs to transition

This section focuses on questions and challenges that arise when a loved one transitions and includes issues about staying together, raising children, and managing a sense of betrayal or abandonment such as "How could you do this to me" or "Did you ever love me?

It is important to remember that your spouse/partner who is transitioning loved you when you got together, and in many cases, still loves you today. You may have a hard time accepting the changes in your partner's transgender or CG identity, however, it has nothing to do with the love s/he has for you.

Every relationship/marriage may not stay as it was because many factors will come into play. The outcome will be impacted by how you create and identify the relationship/marriage. Will you be able to stay together, or will it be the end of the relationship/marriage?

If you stay together, the relationship/marriage will likely need to be redefined and new rules will need to be set. Staying together is a decision you both will have to make while keeping in mind it will be hard work for you both. If you feel you need to separate, this separation does not necessarily mean war. You are both adults and making the process as amicable as possible is critical, especially if a child or children are involved.

If you have children, you are both responsible for them, and remember that children learn from watching you. You and your transgender partner do not need to be close friends through this process or in the future, but you need to be in agreement when it comes to raising children. It is important that, in this endeavor, you work together. Remember to keep in mind what we learned about language and what we learned about behaviour. It is not uncommon that some people have a hard time seeing their ex-spouse/partner in person in their new gender identity. You might agree to communicate via email or through a shared notebook that the children can bring back and forth.

Sometimes, it can be hard on a spouse/partner to admit that s/he actually passes and dresses well and is looking good. We may even have feelings of jealousy. You will need to admit and deal with your own issues of ego, insecurities, and negativity. Remember, anger is due to feeling hurt and how we deal with this pain, whether positively or negatively, can determine whether you will hurt more or less.

Other factors that can challenge a relationship/marriage are the age of the individuals, their individual sexual orientation, and the kind of relationship/marriage they want in the future. We often see in clinic that, if the individuals involved are older, they may be inclined to work it out in order to live together, and also maintain parts of their life which they keep separate. Not surprisingly, financial dependency often plays a significant part in the decision-making.

For some couples, sex plays a less important role; perhaps it was non-existent for years, or perhaps the relationship/marriage is based on friendship and companionship. Often, however, if couples are younger, sex is still an important part of the relationship/marriage. These couples may find that their sexual orientation is not compatible, or that there are no children to consider, or that the non-transitioning spouse wants a child in the future. In these cases, couples may not be able to avoid separation.

In my work with couples, I find that if the relationship/marriage was very good, often it was found through this process that gender did not matter as much to people. Rather, the love and friendship couples carried for their spouse/partner overruled all challenges. Others came to realize that they had always had strong bisexual longings. In these cases, many relationships/marriages overcame great difficulties and couples stayed together.

There are some couples who are able to work out their relationship challenges together, while others need help and find it when they seek couple counselling. If choosing the latter, be sure that your doctor/therapist is above all things, open minded and understanding of diversity.

CG relationships are often very difficult since there can be an unrelenting fear of not knowing who sees you when you leave the house, of not knowing where your spouse/partner goes, and of being seen getting ready for an outing. Can the CG individual go away without creating stress or financial difficulties for the relationship/marriage? There is the consideration that a CG person needs clothing for each gender, such as a wig, make-up, or other things. Many new challenges can create stressors on relationships/marriages. Also, if the individual is not "out," there is a constant purging and buying of clothing, often causing financial strain. For everyone involved, there is the constant question of "Who can I trust?" All of these matters can affect the physical and mental health of everyone involved.

Likely some TG or CG people will have known for a long time "who" they are gender-wise, but others struggle with this question for many years. After coming out, we often see the TG /CG individuals needing to talk about transition and being their "true self." Getting loved ones involved, TG people may forget that their spouses/partners, children, and work mates are finding out this unexpected news for the first time and now need time to adjust. It can often become over-whelming for a non-TG person. Since a TG/CG person has repressed their feelings and waited so long to come out, they forget that their transition is not the only important thing in the world. Indeed, life, work, child/ren, finances, and relationships continue. The TG person is ready, but for everyone else, it's new and often a shock, and they will need time to catch up. Patience on both sides of these relationships is important, and discussions about the issue and how we move on will be required—yet not every day. Life and living are imperative—this helps to adjust and see that the TG/CG individual is still the one you love.

Section 4–Questions and concerns from someone who is questioning their own gender

In this final section, additional questions commonly raised by a trans individual are addressed, including "Do I need to transition?" and "Where do I fit in?"

When we look at TG individuals and those who see a doctor/thera-pist to address these concerns, there are generally two groups. There are those who know what they want when they come to professionals for help. These individuals generally want access to hormones, or if they are already on hormones, they want sex-reassignment-surgery (SRS) and help to get approval for government financial assistance, such as OHIP.

Other TG people come with many questions for their medical or other support professionals, such as "I am not sure if I am TG, and if I am, do I need to transition?" Some others want professionals to make the decision for them. Remember, no one else can make this decision; the TG individual themselves has to make the decision.

Our work as professionals is to help the TG person find their space on the spectrum of gender. When one finds their space on the spectrum, the TG individual is in the driver's seat and their doctor/therapist can now help them to overcome the difficulties that come with transitioning. Achieving a satisfying and positive quality of life should be the final outcome of the transition process.

What is the difference between fixed and fluid?

In research conducted in 2008 (Seidl 2008), I separated the terminology of the gender continuum into two groups. A significant difference between using the gender binary only and the one that was used in the 2008 research was achieved by clustering a variety of gender identities into two groups: fixed or fluid. This created a more inclusive typology for clinical use. The fixed cluster included transgender individuals who preferred the explicit category of either male or female, within a gender binary. The fluid cluster preferred a fluid interpretation, in which gender is experienced as potentially flexible and on a continuum.

I found that this is a very important differentiation that the individual needs to recognize, before boxing themselves into a fixed gender binary. In the cross-gender (CG) population, which falls under the fluid

"At times it will be difficult for the transgender individual and for family, friends, and co-workers to go through transitioning. The process will take patience, understanding, education, and foremost, love and trust in 'trying to get along' and accepting diversity."

"I see individuals in this population as butterflies. At first they are in a cocoon, working hard to come out, which is often a challenging task. My job as doctor/therapist, and the role of family, friends, or co-workers, and other allies, is to be there to assist these beautiful individuals gain their wings and learn to fly."

category, some changes might be needed which are possible and help the individual to have a better quality of life.

For example, help could be in the form of decreasing the levels of the hormone Estrace, or for some FTMs, a hysterectomy (if needed) can be used to stop menstruation. Others might not like visible breasts, and a male chest can be created surgically. Yet, these individuals may not want to take testosterone, change their gender marker or name, or they may wish to switch back and forth, from female to male to female.

For MTFs who may want and or need to be both genders, they may want or need electrolysis or laser treatment. These individuals may need to decrease their testosterone levels a bit to feel more comfortable but also functioning.

Other transgender people feel completely fine with their female or male secondary sex organs and with their full current hormone levels. In this case, the only thing they want is to be comfortable and to switch back and forth between genders and to reach acceptance of being CG.

There is nothing wrong with these categories on the gender spectrum. The importance is for people to recognize what they need, to take their time, and to not be boxed into the gender binary. Even as we get older, peer pressure and our own need of acceptance and fitting in is important and might push some people into making the wrong decision for themselves. Making well-informed decisions is important.

The gender spectrum is open and flexible; some CG individuals may spend their entire life there, while others might move in either direction at a later point in their life. My advice is to be open and accepting to the range of gender expressions on the gender continuum.

Let's address the fixed gender group

As in all groups the most important thing for the fixed gender group is self-recognition and acceptance. It is only after these individuals accept their place on the gender spectrum that they can start to move forward and transition.

Often individuals struggle for a long time with fear of being the only one who has these feelings, being found out, and not being accepted. Like those in the general population, use of negative and self-destructive coping methods such as self-medicating with alcohol and drugs are used by some in this population.

Other coping methods might appear to be less self-destructive, such as daydreaming and fantasizing. However, these can still have a damaging impact on an individual's life. These may bring some relief, but at the same time, it can also get people into trouble. If in school, they may not be participating or may be missing important information in class, and then possibly being used as an example of "bad behaviour" to classmates. When at home or in relationships, daydreaming or fantasizing may manifest in being hermit-like or self-centred, or even being uninterested in their partner and issues. Daydreaming, living in a fantasy world, and being self-absorbed with their own behaviour can be methods of survival for a while, but not indefinitely.

GD is the primary diagnosis for the fixed TG individual. Saying that does not exclude the fluid gender population, many of whom also experience GD. Furthermore, for both groups, the impact of some of these negative coping methods, including guilt, shame, or environmental factors that a transgender individual may experience are so severe that s/he can often struggle with secondary and/or tertiary illnesses. These illnesses can include depression, anxiety, concurrent trauma, post-traumatic stress disorder (PTSD), panic disorder, OCD, and personality disorder. Others in this group may experience eating disorders and physical illnesses such as peptic ulcers, headaches, or hypertension.

The above are only some of the issues, which might have to be addressed before and/or during the transition process. Yet, this does not mean that the individual cannot start transitioning. Some issues may resolve themselves as an individual finds internal peace when their mind and body harmonize.

If the transitioning individual is a younger adult, the issue of egg or sperm storage needs to be addressed before starting hormone treatment. During this process, parents or spouses/partners should be included.

As self-acceptance is reached, the process of egg/sperm storage is accepted or declined, and the process of assessment for the diagnosis of GD has been completed, the next and often desperately anticipated step can finally be addressed.

While I realize that some people do not want to be diagnosed or labelled, a diagnosis is needed if the support of insurance is required.

Hormone treatment

Hormone treatment can be started by your GP, an endocrinologist, or a practical nurse (PN). Some of these professionals will need a letter of recommendation and a GD diagnosis. Others work with the concept of informed consent, explained above.

If a TG individual struggles with enormous amounts of fear "of making the right decision or of being an outcast," and their anxiety and depression is becoming overwhelming, then other steps can be initiated. Starting with blockers (for three to four months) prior to hormones can help decrease anxiety and depression, and enhance the ability to think more clearly, and experience a decrease in testosterone in MTF and estrogen in FTM if it feels right.

At this point, hormones such as Estrace for MTF and testosterone for the FTM can be added in the transition process. The next step in the transition process is to send in the papers for name and gender-marker change. Additionally, the doctor, endocrinologist, or NP who is prescribing hormones needs to write a letter confirming that the individual is on hormones and that their gender marker can now be changed. Remember, this may change as laws change; different provinces in Canada already have differences in the process.

In my practice, I always recommend that clients stop calling themselves transgender. I tell my clients, "You are a female or a male. Confidently introduce yourself in the gender of your true self, and people will find it easier to accept you as they follow your lead." As well, once you feel you have made the right choice for you, and you feel happy and comfortable in your body, the Diagnostic Statistical Manual's (DSM) diagnosis of GD will no longer be relevant. Remember that no one is happy and comfortable in their body every day. We may feel too fat, too skinny, too short, too tall, and on and on, but we do not question our gender on a daily basis as you once did.

As I discussed earlier in the chapter, coming out to family and to children is best only after self-acceptance. In the workplace, it is best to come out when you are ready to start living full-time in your true gender and you have received papers with your new name and gender. In most employment scenarios, talking with your supervisor or HR personnel is the most effective route. Ask them to talk with your co-workers on your behalf. This process could include reading a short letter you have written, talking about your fears, and sharing your new name. (See Chapter 6 for more on transitioning in the workplace.)

The Bathroom

Using bathrooms is another issue that often becomes a struggle for the TG individual. Depending on the stage in the transitioning process, the question often becomes, "What bathroom should I use?" It is often safer to use a single-stall bathroom early in the transition process or hormone treatment. In some areas, the accessibility bathroom might be the only single-stall bathroom available. When people start re-affirming your gender as that which you know is the right gender, then that is the time to use the bathroom of your true gender self. (See Chapter 3 for more on issues around public bathrooms.)

Sex-Reassignment-Surgery (SRS)

Some individuals might want surgery. An MTF may seek Vaginoplasty, and others might want breast augmentation, facial-feminization surgery (FFS), or a tracheal shave for the transition. Others may only want an Orchidectomy.

For the FTM, a mastectomy with male chest reconstruction is often the starting point. Some FTMs find that this is the right place in the transition process and they do not need to go further, while others will want Metoidioplasty or a full Phalloplasty. In these cases, a hysterectomy is needed.

If you wish to have more detail regarding surgery or even hormone treatments, I strongly suggest a talk with your doctor/therapist. There are different types of hormones or types of surgeries available, which go beyond the scope of this book.

How far you want to go in your transition is an individual choice. Whether you are fixed (female or male) or fluid (both), being in your true-gender self is the goal. What is beneath your clothing is no one's business but yours.

Additionally, having contact with others is important in the transition process. In this way, not only is the new gender reaffirmed but also trust can be established. Trust is knowing what to take personally, what is outside of your control, and when to stand up for yourself or let go. New gender behaviour needs to be learned; going through the different developmental stages and growing up and becoming the new self will not happen overnight. It is the same as your physical development—it's a slow process.

At times it will be difficult for the TG individual, as well as for family, friends, and co-workers. The process will take patience, understanding, education, and foremost, love and trust, in "trying to get along" and accept diversity.

In closing

There is so much more to talk about with this complex topic of transgenderism—a part of the greater gender continuum.

The questions raised and the answers provided in this chapter are based on my clinical experience as a gender specialist, but these do not address all the questions, and these answers are not necessarily one-size-fits-all. You will likely have questions based on your own cultural, ethnic, social status, religion, work, and other experiences and personal situations that are unique to you. It is my hope that, in time, you find answers to your questions.

I believe that the discussion about gender is a topic about visibility—being visible, recognized, and accepted in the gender or genders that only you know is right for you. Education can help to alleviate fears, and we need to work together to achieve positive change. Then, and only then, will we be able to ensure that everyone on the gender continuum is included and is a full participant in society.

Finally, allow me to share the following: In my work, I see individuals in this population as butterflies: at first, they are in a cocoon, working hard, and trying to come out which is often difficult. Our job as doctor/therapist, family, friends, co-workers, and allies, is to be there to help them to get their wings and to fly.

CHAPTER 6

Gender transitioning in the workplace

Increasingly, workplaces are becoming safer places for trans and gender non-conforming people. This chapter includes personal anecdotes and perspectives from people who have transitioned while in the workplace, and insights about the impact of those transitions. The chapter also includes information about what is required for workplaces to create safe spaces for gender diversity.

WORKPLACE

Gender transitioning in the workplace

Prior to transition, many of my suggestions or ideas in meetings tended to be accepted readily or at least listened to. Today, I find myself either having to shout a little louder to be heard or being quietly dismissed. I have also noticed that I'm not kept in the loop as much as I used to be, but I accept that. It goes with the territory in this male-dominated organization. My feeling is that this dismissal is not always intentional but likely a product of societal differences between male vs female privilege in the grand scheme of things."

—Jodie (male to female)[21]

Gender differences have played out in workplaces for decades. Historically, the dialogue has focused on the balance—or rather imbalance—of power between men and women regarding markers of success, power, and access. There has been a long history of men dominating women regarding opportunities to be the boss of a company, having a seat at the boardroom table, and raking in higher wages.

The recent winds of politics and the realities of economics have helped to balance things to a degree, but workplace equality between men and women is still very much a work in progress. While this gender-balancing work carries on, a new conversation about gender has emerged in workplaces—and it seems to be getting bolder by the

21   Please note that all personal names used have been changed.

moment. The dialogue is about gender diversity and approaches to creating safe and equitable places where people of all gender expressions and identities can work without harassment, discrimination, or discomfort.

Being successful at work has been, for the most part, about "fitting in." The more you fit comfortably into the culture, the easier your experience to integrate personally and professionally. This is particularly true regarding fitting into the expectations of conventional gender roles of male and female. Trans and gender-nonconforming people are not always an easy fit with conventional gender expressions. They tend to be part of a marginalized group of individuals who identify and express themselves in ways that are outside of the conventional binary male/female majority.

There is no shortage of experiences reported by trans and gender-nonconforming people[22] of discrimination, harassment, unfair treatment, loss of positions, lack of respect, and reduced financial security. Trans people report being fired for being trans, passed over for promotions, and taken off work duties that dealt directly with the public. They report being denied mentoring opportunities, receiving lesser pay for their work, and being socially rejected, othered, and isolated.

There is no clear roadmap for a trans person "coming out" in a workplace that ensures their professional and personal safety. Nor is there a clear roadmap for a comfortable experience for staff and management who work alongside a person who is transitioning. How included, excluded, accepted, discriminated against, or normalized a trans person's experience is in a workplace depends on many factors: the job they hold, the culture of the workplace, the attitudes of leadership, the human rights policies within the organization, and the

22 Jasmin Roy Foundation Report 2017

laws of the city, province, and country. An organization's non-discrimination policies are one thing—how those policies and laws are integrated and practiced is another. I once worked at an organization that prided itself on having accumulated a great many Healthy Workplace accolades. On paper, it all looked great. They seemed to be doing all the right things to create a safe workplace, and the public optics certainly concurred. However, employees in non-conforming minority groups spoke of a different story.

It is in the "lived-in" places that reveal the essence of a workplace culture and their sensitivity to human rights and diversity: the cubicles, kitchens, elevators, boardrooms, and private email streams. How is a trans or gender non-conforming person received and treated and spoken about in these contexts? The degree of acceptance and respect within a culture also shows up in the streams of communication—written, verbal, and non-verbal. Most of us know what the language of disrespect looks and feels like. We know when we are being snubbed or ignored. We know when we are being spoken to with dismissive words or a derogatory tone. We also know

Jodie
(male to female)

One of the biggest challenges in my transition was coming out to my immediate co-workers. I was able to help organize a "diversity day" with various speakers and trans education. I chose not to be present that day so that everyone would have the freedom to ask questions and voice any concerns. I received lots of positive feedback afterwards and this seemed to alleviate many fears and unknowns. I sense there are still a couple of my co-workers who will never accept me in my true gender or understand my need to transition but that's their problem, not mine. As long as they treat me with respect and remain professional, that's all that matters to me.

Kim
(male to female)

What's important is who I am, not what I am.

Heather

(an employer of a trans employee)

At first, it was hard to remember to not misgender him. For those of us on the outside, all we see is what we can see. So, if you have grown up in a time when you assumed someone who looks female is called "she" then it takes real work to change that habit. Randall taught me that it is really important to do that work–that it's a matter of fundamental respect for what your employee needs to feel respected. Randall was very good at politely reminding me and others about what he needed to feel respected–such as not misgendering him. He was understanding of us when we slipped up, and that made a big difference. It's clear he has to stay vigilant–particularly with clients.

the feeling of being accepted, respected, and acknowledged.

Cultural attitudes in a workplace often have a great deal to do with the attitudes and behaviour of senior management. The more support the leadership provides—or is seen to provide—the more accepting staff tend to be towards "normalizing" the integration of a trans person into the workplace.

In my career as a workplace trainer, I have seen evidence of this firsthand. Soon after Skyler started his transition, I began to travel to workplaces across Canada to speak to staff and management about transgender and gender non-conforming identities, and how workplaces can respond in supportive ways through policy and practice.

One of my first training assignments was at a workplace where a senior leader in a high-profile public organization was transitioning from male to female. It was my job to help guide the management to ensure a good experience for the transitioning employee, and to provide training for staff. They all wanted more understanding about their colleague they had known for many years as a male who would be showing up to work the following week as a female. I was also there to support the management team in developing a deeper understanding of gender diversity in general, and to help them navigate the impacts of the employee's transition—with staff, the management team, and the public.

The leadership team of this high-profile public organization was supportive, but they were also completely unprepared for how to manage this shift in dynamics. They wanted everything to go well of course—not only because they had a high public profile but also because they really cared about their fellow senior leader. Michael was a twenty-five-year veteran of the organization who, at the age of fifty, was taking the courageous journey to transition to the female identity she had always felt she was. No one in the workplace had been through this before.

Management wanted all staff and workplace leaders to be on-side and respectful, but it was clear they were not sure what to do, or what *not* do—legally, professionally, or personally. They needed to know what company policy modifications were needed to accommodate Michael's change. How were staff members going to be informed, and how would that go over? How would different reactions be managed? How was this going to play out in the public eye? And what about female staff members? How were they going to feel about having a trans woman use their washroom and change room? The organization had a lot of questions to ask and even more uncertainties they didn't know how to articulate.

My first order of business was to meet with the trans employee before she was scheduled to go on leave. Her intention was to be away from work for about two weeks and then return as the female she had been hiding from public view for most of her fifty years. The employee's hope was that, during her absence, management would sort out all the large and small administrative details, and that staff members would have gained some understanding about the subject of gender diversity.

She hoped that, upon her return, she would be warmly welcomed, be greeted by her new name, Jodie, and addressed with female pronouns. She was looking forward to everyone carrying on business as usual. From her point of view, the only thing that was changing was how she would be showing up to work. With her transition, she could show up every day as her authentic female self and no longer need to pretend to be a man.

One of the key messages that Jodie wanted everyone to hear was that she would still be the same person after her transition. She was still good at her job, and still funny, smart, and personable. The only real difference was that now she was finally happy living in her body.

For many trans people, the message that they want cis people to hear is that transitioning from one gender to another does not change who they are intrinsically. They are the same person, only now they are outwardly living their truth.

I am happy to report that Jodie's workplace transition was a success—thanks to the dedication of the management team to ensure that every single employee attended a training session and was given space to voice any concerns or discomforts related to changes impacting them from the transition of their colleague. Many questions arose during the training sessions, such as, "Is Michael—I mean, Jodie—still going to be able to do his—I mean, her—job?" and "What are we supposed to say to the people who ask where Michael is?" Others wanted to know, "Did she get surgery done?" and "Is she, like, a real woman now?" And of course, "Which bathroom is she going to use?" Often the inevitable comment would arise: "This is just too weird for me."

To these comments, I would emphasize that their colleague's transition was *not* about them (the people asking the questions). It was about Jodie, who used to be known as Michael. My message was direct and straightforward: "This is about her living her own authentic life. It has nothing to do with you."

I also reminded them that "there is no need to change your beliefs or personal values regarding someone who expresses their gender in a way that's different from your own experience. You don't have to accept the idea that someone feels that they are meant to be a different gender than the one they were born into. The single request here is for respectful behaviour. That's it—a request for respect!"

I remember the silence in the room when I clarified that their one job here was to be respectful. I repeated it twice to make sure everyone really heard it. I could hear a collective sigh of relief that I was not asking them to change their beliefs or shift out of their comfort zone. I was appealing to their humanity and simply asking them to behave in respectful ways. Most people were able to accept that request—regardless of their own religious, cultural, political, or social influences.

By the time Jodie returned to work, the organizational training had been completed, new policies were in place, and her personal documentation had been updated by Human Resources. The focus of her attention now was given to navigating the day-to-day interactions of re-integrating as a different gender. Jodie was very reflective:

> "I felt like I was in a kind of limbo between two worlds—not fully accepted by the women, and no longer allowed into the inner circle of the men. I always knew that men had a privileged place, but I realized it so much more when I was no longer a part of it... I so clearly heard the chauvinistic comments by men and saw that they weren't really aware of how they were coming across. The behind-the-scenes locker-room conversation is about girlfriends and wives... lots of jokes and women-bashing. When I point it out, they

tell me, 'You don't understand...We're just joking around.' I end up staying quiet now in conversations. And that has its own problems, because now I often feel excluded from casual conversations at work. The guys don't want to be called on their stuff...They feel threatened by it. They deflect it or just don't take any responsibility for their bashing comments.

"I see how men change their tone when women are around. The air changes. They'll embrace a woman and shake hands with a guy. There are so many subtle changes that people aren't aware of. But the reality—at least in my experience—is that men don't take women as seriously as they do other men. Workplaces just don't operate on the same keel for men and women."

Being addressed accurately was also an aspect of adjustment—for everyone. It didn't come easily for many people to start using a different name and pronoun. Jodie reported that, even a year after her transition, some staff members still used male pronouns to refer to her and even occasionally used her old name.

Changing behaviour takes time. I can certainly attest to the stubbornness of linguistic habits even in my own family. It has been over ten years since Skyler's transition, and yet some friends and family members still ask me, when referring to Skyler and my daughter Lauren, "So how are the girls?" I stay patient and forgiving and say, "You mean, 'How are the kids?'" to which they quickly and apologetically respond back, "Oh sorry, yes...How are the kids?" Changing behaviour indeed takes time.

Over the many years that I have been delivering these messages to workplaces across Canada, I have seen a gradual increase in trans and gender-nonconforming people coming out in workplaces. Currently, there are no stats available to support this observation, but there have been policy changes in the last few years in Canada and around the world that indicate clear support for trans and LGBTQ+ employees. In 2017, the Canadian government implemented Bill C-16 that amended the Human Rights Act to outlaw employment discrimination based on gender identity and expression.[23]

Both the federal and provincial human rights legislations grant protection to trans employees as well as trans job candidates. There are provincial human-rights charters and codes across the country that generally prohibit employers from practicing any form of discrimination based on gender identity or gender expression in an employment context. This protection includes hiring, training, promoting, or terminating a trans person's employment on either of these grounds.[24] As of 2018, ninety-three percent of Fortune 500 companies have

....

23   Human Rights Watch, World Report 2017.
24   See Laurier, Justine, "Preventing and Ending Discrimination and Harassment of Transgender Employees, The Globe and Mail, October 5, 2017, https://www.theglobeandmail.com/report-on-business/careers/leadership-lab/preventing-and-ending-discrimination-and-harassment-of-transgender-employees/article36456796/.

Claire
(male to female)

I feel othered when people stare at me. I'm particularly aware of this when I use a public women's washroom, or when incorrect pronouns are used to refer to me. I feel othered when I don't seem to fit in. Othering is about how other people building walls when I'm trying to bring mine down.

Resa
(male to female)

Transitioning meant an exchange – a loss of privilege in my community in return for personal serenity.

Giselle
(parent of a trans child)

We go through life thinking we are wonderfully progressive people, until we come up to something we can't embrace. Then we need to think about how to embrace it without causing harm.

non-discrimination policies that include sexual orientation, and eighty-five percent have non-discrimination policies that include gender identity.[25] It is also interesting to note that, as of this writing, the US still has no federal law protecting employees from discrimination based on sexual orientation or gender identity.[26]

Success stories of trans people in workplaces hardly ever make the news, yet there are many positive examples of integration, acceptance, and success of trans people thriving, both personally and professionally, in their workplaces. What seems clear from the research and from my personal experience of supporting employee transitions across the country is that the more open this conversation is, that is to say, the more acceptable it is to be able to discuss gender in honest, unguarded ways, the less fear, discrimination, and harassment there will be. This also goes for schools, families, and communities.[27] Scads of research studies have arrived at this conclusion, but really, it seems pretty obvious that the safer people feel at speaking about gender differences, the healthier the environment.

Harassment and discrimination

Despite the increased awareness, education, and policies that exist to promote awareness and support, trans and gender-nonconforming people can still experience marginalization in their workplace.

Harassment is a dark and difficult behaviour that can show up as threats, leering, assault, circulating hurtful information or photos, or

25 Corporate Equality Index, "Rating Workplaces on Lesbian, Gay, Bisexual, Transgender, and Queer Equality" (2019) https://www.hrc.org/campaigns/corporate-equality-index.

26 Julie Moreau, NBC News 2019; USA Today, posted Oct 19, 2019.

27 Trans PULSE, 2012.

inappropriate touching. It is a bullying tactic that is meant to ridicule, ostracize, or exert power over someone. Another bullying tactic is the use of microaggressions: subtle comments or actions that are hostile, derogatory, insensitive, or just plain unkind. Microaggressions in the workplace can be as direct as treating someone as though they were invisible, or as indirect as not including them on a team email list.

Discrimination may take many forms and can also be both indirect and direct. Indirect discrimination can be carried out through another person or organization so that there is no single person taking accountability for the inequitable behaviour. Direct discrimination can feel like bullying or intimidation, being denied a promotion, being moved to a position with lower responsibility or reduced visibility to the public, or even dismissal from employment.

Important questions to ask ourselves, our work groups, and our leadership are: How can we ensure that workplaces are safe and supportive for everyone? What do we need to do so that trans and gender non-conforming employees receive the same job opportunities that cis employees get? How can we help educate ourselves and others

Claire
(male to female)

My experience at work has been amazing. My work fully supported me as I came out. The compassion and understanding from my co-workers have shown me that I am valued as much for my contribution to work as for being authentic to myself.

Jodie
(male to female)

Reflecting on the differences I've noticed at work between my pre- and post- transition, I would say that most of the differences have been subtle. That may be because people know that any overt transphobic discrimination is grounds for termination. On rare occasions where I have had a disagreement with a co-worker or a manager, I tried to stay professional–regardless of whether I felt they were coming from a place of transphobia or just a difference of opinion.

Claire
(male to female)

Being trans or acting on feeling trans is not a choice. People think it is but it's not. I have experienced more pain in my life by this one judgement. I wouldn't choose an identity crisis or wish it on my enemies. It's not a choice or a lifestyle or a fetish. It's who I am – the essential me. If I have made any choice (I have to admit this word carries a lot of pain with it) it's that I'm choosing honesty, authenticity and to say that I'm worth being loved by me. Everyone should be able to say to themselves they are worth it, and if they can't they're hiding something from themselves.

Sandra
(male to female)

I went from a closeted, miserable person to someone who sees the possibility of a healthier future.

so that gender-diverse people are treated in a normalized way, and not made to feel unwelcome or uncomfortable?

When, how, or if a trans person comes out in their workplace is a very personal and intentional consideration. Cis people generally have a more casual, or at least unconscious, approach to their gender identity. They "out" themselves without giving it a second thought. Consider the social chatter in an office. Cis people openly talk about their partner, the public activities they share, the clothes they buy, and the myriad aspects of their personal life. Just casual talk. When you are part of the majority population, social conversation can be easy. In majority populations, there is no need to consciously self-edit to keep one's true identity secret and safely hidden from public awareness.

For those outside the majority, however, this casual banter requires keen attention. High alert questions are always being considered:

» Is it a safe environment in which to come out and identify myself?

» If others find out who I really am, will I lose my job, my co-worker relationships, my status, or my benefits?

» If I come out, will I get support from my management?

» Will there be gossip?

» Will I be harassed?

» Will I be treated with respect?

» Will I be given the right to use the washroom and change room that corresponds to the gender I identify with?

» Will I be able to dress in ways that express the gender I identify with?

» Will I feel safe—emotionally, physically, and professionally?

These are questions that would likely never occur to a cisgender person in the workplace, and yet these are the questions that are in the forefront of a trans person's mind long before they make decisions about coming out at work.

In a workplace that operates with a culture of respect towards diversity, employees likely have a shared understanding of the expectations regarding behaviours of inclusion and respect. When there is shared understanding, communication is more comfortable. Without comfortable communication, difficult behaviours can arise such as avoidance, conjecture, gossip, offensive comments or behaviour, and curiosity that can invade privacy. When people are not sure how to behave or are not clear about what is and is not appropriate, the stress of uncertainty can lead to offensive behaviour.

Considerations for creating a respectful workplace culture

Each and every person in a workplace has the power to inspire others in that workplace to behave in respectful and supportive ways. Those in official leadership positions often have a more significant impact since they can set the tone and model behaviour in public ways. It is not, however, only the impact of leadership or the policies in place that establish the tone of the workplace—it is the overall culture.

A workplace culture is a combination of everything and everyone. When it comes to gender diversity, there are key culture-based questions to ask:

» Is your workplace safe enough for a trans or gender-nonconforming employee to disclose their gender identity?

» Will they feel safe and supported?

» Will co-workers be respectful in their attitudes and behaviours towards this person?

» Will accommodations be made for washroom and change rooms?

» If anyone is uncomfortable with the changes, will their concerns be heard and addressed?

When it comes to supporting trans or gender-nonconforming employees, the goal in workplaces, as the Canadian government says, is to work together "in a spirit of

Sandra
(male to female)

On a professional level, I find that I am more frequently treated the way that I have heard many other women complain about in professional settings. I am now more likely to get talked over or interrupted. Some people even think I no longer have the same technical skills and knowledge I had before I transitioned. I am now no longer expected to be able to explain new processes about hardware or software. On the other side of things, I am also no longer expected to provide frequent out-of-office support and that means I can maintain a better work/life balance.

Sandra
(male to female)

Before I transitioned, I was good at what I do, and now I'm still good at what I do.

openness, honesty and transparency that encourages engagement, collaboration and respectful communication."[28] Imagine if all workplaces operated like this!

A guide for doing the right things

The following is a guide for developing workplace policies, procedures, behaviours, and attitudes that help create and sustain a culture of openness, honesty, and respectfulness.

Ensure personal privacy and confidentiality

» Organizations can collect personal information only if it has a specific purpose. Once collected, this information needs to be kept private and confidential.

» It is legally unacceptable as well as inappropriate to disclose personal and confidential information about a person's gender identity and sexual orientation. Any communication about such personal information requires the agreement of the individual. Beyond the legal duty to keep a person's private information private, disclosing this information can, in some cases, expose them to discrimination, harassment, or even danger.

» Organizations need to tell employees where their personal data will be stored, who will have access to it, what they intend to do with it, and what confidentiality and privacy protections are involved in the data collection.

....

28   Government of Canada, Public Services and Procurement, "Support for Trans Employees: A Guide for Employees and Managers," https://www.tpsgc-pwgsc.gc.ca/apropos-about/guide-et-te-eng.html.

Use requested names and pronouns

» Every effort needs to be made by everyone in the organization to use the person's preferred name and pronouns in daily interactions. All workplace communication and documentation also need to reflect a person's preferred way be being addressed.

Provide gender inclusive washrooms and change rooms

» Every employee has the right to use the washroom that corresponds to the gender they identify with. Some changes to the available facilities may be required to accommodate a trans employee so that all employees are comfortable. If a washroom is single-stalled, one option for making this accommodation is to shift the washroom from "male/female" to "gender neutral."

» For an employer, the essential thing is to be openly communicative with the staff about the trans employee's change of washroom usage. Management should ensure that all employees are aware of and comfortable with, or at least tolerant of, the changes proposed. Any proposed change to the use of facilities needs to be communicated to all employees before any change is implemented so that everyone will have an opportunity to express their concerns or questions.

» It is important to create a Transition Plan that outlines how and when the trans employee will inform the others in the workplace. Whether the employee discloses first to Human Resources, to their manager, or to a member of the leadership team, a plan should include the following:

- Set a date for the announcement of name and pronoun change.

  · Create a plan for how staff will be informed. Consider if that will take place in groups, individually, or by a letter written by the trans person and emailed.

  · Provide information sessions that include opportunities to ask questions.

- Update staff about any change in use of washroom facilities and address questions or concerns.

- Ensure that the health and safety policies have been updated to reflect the inclusion of gender rights. Distribute the updated policies.

  · Communicate expectations of respectful behaviour.

Use words and phrases that demonstrate respect

» Do not use the terms "trans" or "transgender" as a noun; it is objectifying and not appropriate to say, for example, "she's a transgender" or "she's a trans."

» Do not use the term "trans" or "transgender" as a verb; it is inappropriate to say, "he transgendered." Use "transitioned" instead.

» Use the name that a trans person asks you to use; do not refer to them by their birth or legal name if they have specified a different name.

» Use the pronouns that a trans person uses to identify themselves (she/her; he/him; they/them).

» Use gender neutral pronouns (they, them) to be respectful of all gender diversity.

» Do not use the term "biologically male" or "biologically female," or refer to a trans person as being "born a male" or being "born a female" to identify their gender; use the term "their sex assigned at birth."

» Do not use the term "sex change;" use the term "transition."

» When referring to surgeries, use the term "sex reassignment surgery" (SRS).[29] Please note, however, that asking someone about their medical procedures without first getting their consent is inappropriate in most impersonal contexts, such as at work. Discussions regarding SRS are to be conducted only with the trans person's healthcare professional and loved ones.

» Do not use any language that is offensive or derogatory to identify a trans or gender-nonconforming person.

» Use the term "trans man" to refer to someone who has transitioned from female to male; use the term "trans woman" to refer to someone who has transitioned from male to female.

» The term "trans" is often used as an umbrella term to identify the spectrum of gender-nonconforming people, including: agender, bigender, genderqueer, genderfluid, trans women, and trans men.

» Offensive jokes relating to someone's gender identity or sexual orientation are a form of harassment.

» If you are not sure of someone's pronouns, politely ask them. (For more on the use of respectful words and terms, see Chapter 7.)

....

29   You might also hear the term gender reassignment surgery. The accurate term is sex reassignment surgery which refers to a physical intervention; gender reassignment refers to the choice a person has made regarding the gender they feel most authentically identifies them.

Clarify expectations of appropriate and inappropriate interactions

» It is inappropriate and invasive to ask about someone's medical procedures or medical history; respect the privacy of others.

» It is completely inappropriate to ask about someone's genitalia.

» It is incorrect to assume that all trans people have had, or will have, surgical procedures.

» Respect the confidentiality of others; it is inappropriate to share someone's medical information without permission from them.

» Do not engage in gossip (i.e., talking about someone without them being present).

» Do not communicate your conjectures (for example your opinions on transgenderism based on incomplete information).

Amy
(male to female)

Workplace gossip happens. I get that. I just want people to be respectful.

Jodie
(male to female)

I've noticed that since my transition, a couple of the men I have worked with for years don't speak to me much anymore. I'm not sure why. Perhaps they either don't want to inadvertently say something to offend me, or maybe they simply have no clue how to have a meaningful conversation with me any longer. I also wonder if it just makes them uncomfortable to be in the company of a trans woman.

Cam
(female to male)

What people think of me is none of my business, but how they treat me is.

Identity respectful and non-respectful behaviours

» When referring to a trans person from an historical perspective—that is, prior to their transition—use the name and pronoun they currently use, *not* their pronoun and name assigned at birth.

» Be aware of any bias you may have toward someone who is trans or gender-nonconforming, and use this self-awareness to ensure that you do not use offensive language, tone, or behaviour—consciously or unconsciously, intended or unintended.

» Recognize that gender identity is separate from sexual orientation; do not make any assumptions about any aspect of a person.

Comments from Dr. Helma on transitioning in a workplace

When the news of a person's transition is announced, the trans person should not be in the room to allow everyone to speak freely without judgement. As the saying goes, the elephant will be out of the room, and when the trans employee returns to work, most people will try their best to use the right name and pronouns. The trans employee will also need to work with their colleagues by showing some understanding if mistakes are made. There may be some people who will not accept these changes. They may feel the need to go to their supervisor to deal with these and other situations to the satisfaction of all parties. Many of my transgender clients have told me that they did not need to address the issue of non-acceptance from a co-worker because other co-workers were dealing with these individuals, and it solved itself in a short time.

CHAPTER 7

Helpful words and phrases

Here you will find words, phrases, and meanings to help you feel more informed about and comfortable with the language of gender diversity. What does transgender actually mean? What does it mean when someone says they're 'gender fluid'? Is 'queer' a derogatory term?

Helpful words and phrases

> "There are profound reasons for why the language that trans people use to describe ourselves and our community's changes and evolves so quickly. In Western culture, non-trans people have for centuries created the language that describes us, and this language has long labeled us as deviant, criminal, pathological, unwell, and/or unreal."

—Alex Kapitan, *The Radical Copyeditor's Style Guide for Writing about Transgender People*[30]

If you are feeling uncertain or unclear about what words to use and what words *not* to use, rest assured that you are not alone. Admittedly, knowing how to talk about trans issues is not always straightforward. Terminology around gender diversity is new for most people. Language is constantly evolving. Words and their direct and indirect meanings continually change to reflect shifting social attitudes. Even the most informed and well-intentioned of us sometimes struggle with finding the right language around gender topics.

As I write this book, many years after my first introduction to my child's gender questioning, I recognize how my own language has changed to reflect new learning. I now use the word "transitioning" instead of "transgendering," and I speak about the "gender spectrum" to refer to the range of gender possibilities. I use the word "binary" to talk

---

30 Alex Kapitan, "The Radical Copyeditor's Style Guide for Writing about Transgender People," August 31, 2017, https://radicalcopyeditor.com/2017/08/31/transgender-style-guide/.

about the social construct of male and female, and the term "cis gender" to talk about the group of people who don't question their gender identity. I have more language and deeper thinking around the meanings of sex and gender than ever before. I am discovering that, with my new vocabulary, I can express myself in ways that are in step with the social politics. And I am happy to report that now I unintentionally offend others way less often—although I must admit that my success with this is still a work in progress.

Being conscious of the words we use regarding topics surrounding gender takes vigilance. Our words reflect our inner dialogue—our thoughts, ideas, emotions, judgements, and unconscious biases. How we use words becomes a habit of communication—and habits can be hard to break. Some language habits actually *need* to be broken and changed, particularly when they involve using words that can be hurtful, dismissive, or disrespectful—no matter how unintended that outcome may be. Consciously and willingly stepping into current word usage for discussions about gender diversity conveys a sense of respect for ideas and people.

There are also many other reasons to pay close attention to the words we use to talk about trans populations and gender identities. One of my own personal pet peeves is the use of the words "problem" or "issue" when talking about gender identities. Being transgender is *not* a problem, nor is it an issue, any more than being female or male is a problem or an issue. There is nothing broken here. Nothing needs to be fixed. The problems lie in how trans people are treated, how they are stigmatized, and how attitudes can sometimes show up as discrimination, harassment, or violence. Problems can also arise when a person is *seen* to be different, or even *perceived* to be different in some way and made to feel uncomfortable or unwanted because of it.

What *is* important in this language arena is to ensure that the words you use are free of judgement and/or discrimination. If you are not sure about someone's pronouns, ask them. If you are not sure about whether a word is appropriate, ask for feedback. Also consider checking out published resources on the subject so that the onus for providing information does not always fall on the people that you are curious about. The key is to be respectful, stay open to learning, and ask for feedback or direction when you are uncertain about what to say.

The following is a glossary of words and phrases that you may find useful in navigating the language around gender diversity. This is by no means a complete list. It is, however, a good start in helping to demystify many of the ideas and words that are now in use and a part of the broadening public conversation about gender.

agender: Agender people, also called genderless, gender-free, non-gendered, or ungender people, are those who identify as having no gender, or being without any gender identity. This category includes a very broad range of identities that do not conform to traditional gender norms.

ally: In the context of gender politics and social justice, an ally is a person who considers themselves a friend to the LGBTQIA+ (see below for definition) community. Allies recognize that the community thrives best with caring supporters, whether they are from the community or not. In general, to be an ally is to think, act, and speak in ways that show respect for others; in this context, it is those in the LGBTQIA+ community. If you are in this community—or any other community—you likely want to surround yourself with people who make you feel safe and supported, particularly if there is the added component of marginalization. Allies are supporters with the intention of providing safe spaces, encouraging equality, and behaving in ways that demonstrate respect, caring, and acceptance.

androgen insensitivity syndrome: Androgen insensitivity syndrome (AIS) is when a person who is genetically male (meaning one who has an X and a Y chromosome) is resistant to male hormones, otherwise known as androgens. A person with AIS has some or all of the physical traits of a female but the genetic make-up of a male.

asexual: Asexuality (or non-sexuality) is the lack of sexual attraction to anyone, or low or absent interest in sexual activity.

bisexual: Being bisexual is when one has romantic or sexual attraction toward both males and females, or romantic or sexual attraction to people of any sex or gender identity. (*see also* pansexual)

blending: The term "blending" speaks to the process of presenting oneself in a way that does not draw attention to possible differences. Blending can allow a person to "fit in," so to speak.

In relation to gender, blending can provide a sense of safety. It can also create an internal struggle between true self-expression and access to a broader social acceptability.

cis, cisgender: "Cis" is a prefix derived from the Latin meaning, "on this side of" (the opposite of "trans" meaning "across from" or "on the other side of"). Cisgender refers to people who feel aligned with the gender they were assigned at birth, meaning the gender noted on their birth certificate. Comprising the majority of the population, cis people typically do not question their gender identity.

coming out: This phrase has become popular within the LGBTQIA+ community to describe someone who identifies to themselves and/or to others that the nature of their sexual orientation is outside of the construct of hetero normativity. This also applies to people who identify to themselves and/or to others that their gender identity does not completely resonate with the gender they were assigned at birth.

discrimination: This is a broadly used term to identify when a person feels negatively impacted by the treatment of others through actions and/or words. In the context of gender diversity, discrimination refers to the experience of feeling stigmatized or negatively impacted because of one's gender identity or gender expression. Discrimination can be direct and obvious, or it can be subtle and hidden. Whether it's intentional or not, discrimination is usually harmful just the same. Discrimination can also occur on a deep systemic level, showing up in organizational rules or policies. Often at the root of discrimination are narrowly viewed social stereotypes about gender, as well as prejudice or fear towards people who identify or express themselves outside the conventional male/female norms.

facial feminization surgery (FFS) or facial masculinization surgery: This type of surgery involves the feminization or masculinization of facial features.

female to male (FTM): FTM is a person who is assigned female at birth but who identifies more towards male on the gender spectrum. Each person will take a different set of actions to embody their authentic gender expression; some will take no action. Regardless of any changes made, the FTM experience speaks to feeling that the female gender assigned at birth is not accurate. (*see Chapter 2 for more information about the stages of transition*)

gay: The word "gay" has come to refer primarily to homosexual men (males who are attracted to same-sex partners). Lesbians (women attracted to same-sex partners) may also be referred to as gay. The word was originally used to mean "carefree," "bright," or "showy" and gradually shifted in the mid-1900s to its current usage. Being gay is not exclusive to cisgender populations. Trans people, for example, can identify as gay.

gender attribution: Gender attribution is the process by which a society assigns or ascribes a gender and/or sex onto a person with or without (usually without) knowing concretely what sex that person is or what gender they identify as[31].

gender binary: This phrase identifies the concept that there are only two categories of gender: male and female. The gender binary is now considered more a mindset than a reality—that is, a social construct. Since the majority of people fit into either the male or female category, the concept of the gender binary has become the accepted "reality" for many cultures. This construct of labeling everyone as either "male" or "female" involves identifying gender roles in ways that stereotype them with expectations of behaviours, interests, clothing choices, professional endeavours, and countless other aspects. The following are types of non-binary genders: agender, bigender, genderfluid, genderqueer, non-binary, and more. (*see "non-binary gender" for more on gender identities*)

gender dysphoria: Gender dysphoria is a condition that describes the experience a person has when the gender they were assigned at birth does not match the gender they feel is authentic to them. Dysphoria is a feeling of anxiety, stress, and intense discomfort. People experiencing

....

31   Toward a Theory of Gender, Kessler & McKenna)

this mismatch (which sometimes includes feeling a mismatch to their genitals) used to be considered by the medical professional as being mentally ill, and considered to have a "gender identity disorder." In 2013, with the release of the *Diagnostic and Statistical Manual of Mental Disorders*, fifth edition (DSM-5), this diagnosis was reclassified, signalling that the medical profession no longer considered gender-nonconformity as a mental illness. The current medical position is that it is the stress, anxiety, and possible depression associated with the mismatch of gender identification and gender identity that is the issue, rather than the person themself. This shift in the DSM's recognition has been a significant support in helping to reduce the stigma around gender-nonconformity.

gender diverse: This phrase is an umbrella term to describe an ever-evolving array of labels that people may apply when their gender identity, expression, or even perception does not conform to the norms and stereotypes that exist. Gender diversity is a part of human nature. It cannot be quantified.

gender expression: Gender expression is a term referring to how a person publicly and/or privately chooses to present their gender. Expression can include an array of physical manifestations, such as the choice of clothing, hairstyles, etc., to a range of mannerisms, such as the tones and intonations of voice, body language, etc. Choosing names and pronouns is also part of gender expression.

genderfluid: Someone who is genderfluid generally does not identify with being either fully male or female. Rather, they identify with a mix of genders combined at the same time or in flux from day-to-day.

A genderfluid person may feel most comfortable using the pronoun "they" to reflect the fluctuations of their gender identity.

gender identity: Gender identity is complex. It not only speaks to the gender we were assigned at birth but also speaks to the gender we want to feel most comfortable expressing. Sometimes, genitals, behaviours, and other gender markers associated with the gender assigned to us at birth do not reflect the gender we identify with. People whose gender identity does not match their biology may choose to transition to the gender they feel most comfortable with.

genderqueer: Genderqueer refers to a person whose gender does not match society's expectations of conventional expressions of male or female. (*see also* queer)

gender-neutral: This term is most commonly used as an adjective, such as in reference to public bathrooms and the use of language. A gender-neutral bathroom is one that is available to everyone without denoting a specific male or female usage. Gender-neutral language aims to be completely inclusive of all genders and avoids identifying or matching gender with social roles.

gender-nonconforming: This term refers to the degree to which a person expresses their gender in nonconventional ways, outside of the socially accepted conventions of masculine or feminine expression. Someone who identifies as gender-nonconforming will dress or behave in ways that do not "fit" with conventional gender expectations. This is not about them being confused; rather, it is about them expressing their essential selves. Gender-nonconformity applies to anyone who feels they do not fit in with conventional male/female gender expressions. Fortunately, gender identities outside of the binary are increasingly being recognized in legal, medical, and psychological systems, as well as in diagnostic classifications. Other similar phrases that identify someone's nonconventional gender identification are "gender variant," "gender atypical," and "genderqueer."

gender transitioning: *see* transitioning

gender variance: Gender variance (also called "gender nonconformity") is an umbrella term that describes gender identities, expressions, or behaviours that are outside the conventionally accepted "norms" of masculine or feminine. People who exhibit gender variance may be called "gender variant," "gender nonconforming," "gender diverse," "gender atypical," or "genderqueer," and may be variant in their gender identity, such as being transgender. The term is not a synonym for transgender, however, and should only be used if someone self-identifies as gender-nonconforming. (*see also* gender-nonconforming)

harassment: This is a form of discrimination. In the context of transgenderism and gender-nonconformity, much like in other marginalized groups, harassment can include sexually explicit or other inappropriate comments, questions, jokes, and/or name-calling, as well as the sending of inappropriate or hurtful images, emails, and social media messages. Harassment also includes transphobia and homophobia, as well as non-consensual sexual advances, touching, and other unwelcome and ongoing behaviours. Harassment is intended to insult, demean, harm, and/or threaten a person in some way.

heterosexism: This term refers to the assumption, expressed overtly or covertly, that all people are, or should be, heterosexual. It is often a subtle form of oppression that reinforces silence and invisibility for people who are gay, lesbian, bisexual, or transgender.

heterosexual: A person who is sexually attracted to people of the opposite sex. Someone who is heterosexual is commonly referred to as "straight." Heterosexuality is a category of sexual orientation, the others being homosexuality, bisexuality, pansexuality, asexuality, and more.

—Traditionally, heterosexuality has referred to the coupling of cisgender men with cisgender women. However, how a couple is perceived may not necessarily be an accurate representation of how they self-identify regarding their sexual orientation and/or gender identity. Not all people who appear to be heterosexual are.

heterosexual privilege: This term refers to the unrecognized and assumed privilege of the significant majority of the population that is heterosexual. Public activities such as holding hands, kissing in public without fear, and talking openly about their partners in social gatherings are all available to heterosexual people without reprisal. This is not necessarily the case for those of other sexual orientations.

homosexual: Traditionally, this term refers to those who have romantic attraction, sexual attraction, or sexual behaviour between members of the same sex or gender. Homosexuality is one of the categories of sexual orientation. Given that gender identity and sexual orientation are separate, homosexuality is not limited to cis gender people.

intersectionality: Intersectional theory takes into consideration the convergence and overlapping of different aspects of one's life, which can result in them experiencing disadvantage or oppression. Such aspects can include race, class, gender identity, sexual orientation, religion, and other identity markers. Singular or multiple sources of being disadvantaged can converge to create oppressive and discriminatory behaviour such as racism, sexism, homophobia, transphobia, or xenophobia.

intersex: Intersex people are born with any number of variations of sex characteristics, including chromosomes, gonads, sex hormones, or genitals that do not fit the typical definitions for male or female bodies. Intersex is not an abnormality or a disorder.

lesbian: The word lesbian has come to refer primarily to homosexual women attracted to same-sex partners. Lesbians may also be referred to as gay. Being lesbian is not exclusive to cisgender women. Trans women, for example, can be lesbian.

LGBTQIA+: This acronym has become a recognizable shorthand to identify the spectrum of sexual orientations and gender identities. It includes all those on the spectrum of sexual orientations and gender identities. The letters of the acronym represent the following: L – lesbian; G – gay; B – bisexual; T- transgender; Q – queer (an umbrella term for sexual and gender minorities who are neither heterosexual nor cisgender) and questioning (this is in recognition that some people are uncertain about their sexual orientation and/or gender orientation); I – intersex; A – asexual; the plus sign (+) refers to the increasing number of sexual orientations and gender identities being identified.

As of the writing of the book, all the letters include: LGBTQQIP2SAA: lesbian, gay, bisexual, transgender, queer, questioning, intersex, pansexual, two-spirit, asexual, and allies. "Allies" is an important recognition, acknowledging that the community thrives best with supporters, although they need not be directly a part of the community itself. "A" can also refer to androgynous. (Note that this acronym is continually changing to reflect the evolving language of gender diversity and the differing opinions and voices being expressed in this arena.)

male to female (MTF): MTF is a person who is assigned male at birth but who identifies more towards female on the gender spectrum. Each person will take a different set of actions to embody their authentic gender expression; some will take no action. Regardless of any changes made, the MTF experience speaks to feeling that the male gender assigned at birth is not accurate. (*see Chapter 2 for more information about the stages of transition*)

marginalization: Marginalization is about social exclusion. This can take place through a set of actions and processes that limit the rights and perceived importance of individuals and/or groups. The result is that the needs, desires, and expectations of marginalized individuals or groups are ignored, and the members are excluded from participating with more dominant groups. Historically, people have been marginalized for reasons of race, gender, ethnicity, and sexual orientation, as well as social, political, and/or economic factors.

misgendering: Misgendering occurs when someone refers to a person or uses language to describe a person that does not align with the gender to which they identify. This can occur both intentionally or unintentionally. For people who are transgender, non-binary, or gender-nonconforming, being addressed by the gender they identify with is both affirming and respectful. Intentional misgendering takes place when someone is deliberate about not acknowledging that someone has transitioned from one gender to another, and continues to call them by their outdated pronoun or name. Unintentional misgendering can occur when someone's gender identity does not match conventional expectations of masculine or feminine. This can—and does—happen frequently to people who may be in early stages of transitioning, pre-transition, or to those who choose not to pursue medical or physical procedures. (see Chapter 3 for more about the impacts of misgendering in public spaces)

out: To "out" someone is to disclose their sexual orientation or gender identity without their consent. It raises issues of privacy and can cause harm.

pangender: Pangender people are those who feel they identify as all genders. The term has a great deal of overlap with genderqueer. Because of its all-encompassing nature, presentation and pronoun usage varies between different people who identify as pangender.

pansexual: A pansexual person is open to romantic and/or sexual experiences with people of all sexes, genders, and gender identities, including those who are bisexual, transgender, androgynous, and genderfluid. Being pansexual is not the same as being polyamorous; pansexuality is about being attracted to people across and within the spectrum of gender identities and expressions; polyamory is about the ability to form romantic and/or sexual relationships with more than one person.

passing: In the context of gender, "passing" applies to those who present themselves in a way that others perceive them to be cisgender—whether this is intentional or not. Passing can look like fitting into cultural expectations of conventional "male" or "female" expressions. Sometimes people refer to "passing" as "flying under the radar." (*see also* blending)

pronouns: Pronouns (e.g., "she," "he," "they") are verbal communication markers that acknowledge a person's gender, in the same way that calling someone by their correct name acknowledges their identity. Pronouns are an ever-evolving aspect of language; it is important to stay informed. Some pronouns that have emerged in the LGBTQIA+ populations include: they/ them/ theirs (in the plural or singular); ze or zie (pronounced like "zee") replaces she/ he/ they; hir/hirs (pronounced like "here") replaces her/hers, him/his, or them/theirs.[32] (*see Chapter 2 for more on pronouns*)

queer: Queer is the "Q" in the LGBTQIA+ acronym. The original meaning of queer was "strange" or "peculiar" and was a pejorative, derogatory label referring to anyone who presented themselves as being outside of the conventional expressions of masculine or feminine, or heterosexuality. The term "queer" was reclaimed by the LGBTQ community in the 1980s as a term of pride, to acknowledge someone's living outside of the conventional binary options of gender expression. The term remains controversial, with some members of the community still considering it as derogatory, while others use it as an umbrella term to reference the larger community of diverse sexual and gender orientations. It can be used as both a noun and an adjective.

questioning: The questioning of one's gender, sexual identity, sexual orientation, or all three is a process of exploration to connect oneself with a more authentic self-identification. People who are "questioning" are still exploring their social/sexual/gender labels for themselves, feeling that these labels may differ from the one assigned at birth or assumed within social construct.

sex: Sex refers to the classifications of male, female, or intersex assigned at birth. Sex is different from gender: Sex is our biological classification, and gender is how we identify with that classification.

....

32   The internet is a vast resource with many sites to explore pronouns. Here is one comprehensive site: see https://www.mypronouns.org

sexual orientation: Sexual orientation is a term used to describe one's pattern of emotional, romantic, and/or sexual attraction. Sexual orientation may include sexual attraction to the same gender (homosexuality), attraction to a gender opposite to your own (heterosexuality), attraction to both male and female (bisexuality), attraction to all genders (pansexuality), or having no feelings of sexual attraction at all (asexuality). Gender identification and sexual orientation are often thought of as the same thing, but they are different aspects of us. One's gender identity is completely separate from one's sexual orientation.

straight: Commonly, "straight" refers to heterosexual cisgender people who are attracted to cis people of the opposite sex. However, there are some trans people who are attracted to people of the opposite sex and who consider themselves to be "straight" because they don't identify themselves as being "queer." As mentioned above (see sexual orientation), gender identity is completely separate from one's sexual orientation.

transgender, trans: Transgender is an umbrella term referring to people with diverse gender identities and expressions that differ from the gender that they were assigned at birth.

trans ally: A trans ally is someone who is supportive of people who may have gender identities or presentations that are nonconforming, fluid, or those who have transitioned from one gender binary to another. (*see also*, ally)

transition/transitioning: In relation to gender, transitioning refers to the process that a person engages in to align themselves with their authentic gender identity, after they recognize that their gender identification differs from the one they were assigned at birth. Not all trans people decide to change their external presentation of gender. A person who self-identifies as trans is trans regardless of any transition process.

trans man: A person who was assigned female at birth and identifies closer to male on the gender spectrum is a trans man. Regardless of any transitioning process, a person who identifies as a trans man is still a trans man. Likely, they will want to be addressed with the male or neutral pronouns such as "he/him," or "they/them."

trans woman: A person who was assigned male at birth and identifies closer to female on the gender spectrum is a trans woman. Regardless of any transitioning process, a person who identifies as a trans woman is still a trans woman. Likely, they will want to be addressed with the female or neutral pronouns such as "she/her," or "they/them."

transphobia: The word "transphobia" is a compound made up of "trans" (the Latin prefix meaning "across" or "the other side of") and "phobia" (the Greek word for "fear"). Transphobia implies a prejudice towards trans and non-gender conforming populations and can be expressed through a range of negative attitudes, feelings, or actions. Transphobia is a specific form of discrimination. The word was added to the *Oxford English Dictionary* in 2013, together with "trans person," "trans man," and "trans woman."[33]

transsexual: No longer a common term, "transsexual" was once used to refer to people who identify with a gender different from the one assigned to them at birth. Although some people still identify with this term, currently the more widely used word is "transgender."

....

33 "New Words List June 2013," *Oxford English Dictionary*, https://public.oed.com/updates/new-words-list-june-2013/.

two-spirit: "Two-spirit" refers to a person who identifies as having both a masculine and a feminine spirit. The term is used by some indigenous peoples to describe their sexual, gender, and/or spiritual identities. As an umbrella term, it may encompass a wide variety of gender identities and sexual orientations, including those who might be described as gay, lesbian, bisexual, pansexual, transgender, genderqueer, or those who have multiple gender identities.

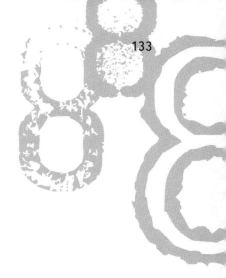

CHAPTER 8

A Useful Approach to Connecting with Resources

By Dr. Helma Seidl, PhD, MSW, RSW, Psychotherapist

Instead of offering a list of resources, which may not be applicable to your location, this chapter offers a host of questions to consider to help you along the path of inquiry in finding the right resource to address your questions, concerns, and needs.

RESOURCES

A Useful Approach to Connecting with Resources

Finding the right resources can be a challenging process since there are many factors to consider. Often people don't know where to start or where to go, and this can create even more anxiety in taking the first step. We hope that this information will help make this first step easier.

When you consider a doctor, nurse practitioner, psychologist, social worker, or psychotherapist (with a minimum of a master's degree), remember that you have the right to ask questions.

The fees may be an issue and so seeing a private psychologist, psychotherapist, or social worker may not be affordable. You might consider a community health centre in your area. Many employ psychotherapists or social workers. The regulations are the same for both private clinics and for public community centres. The difference is cost: A community centre may not charge any fee or may have a sliding fee scale. Some community centres work with the concept of informed consent, explained in Chapter 5.

There are many questions to consider:

» What are the credentials of a practitioner?

» Are they comfortable working with a transgender individual?

» Have they worked with transgender individuals before, and if so, for how many years?

» Are they familiar with the World Professional Association for Transgender Health Standards of Care (WPATH)?

» Have they done gender dysphoria (GD) assessments?

» Are they qualified to write hormone start and/or surgery recommendation letters, and have they done that before?

» Do they work with doctors who specialize in hormone therapy?

» Do they work with doctors who specialize in sex-reassignment-surgery (SRS)?

» Are they a member of and in good standing with their professional association?

Questions of cost need to be clear and straightforward:

» What is the cost of the session?

» What is included in a session?

» How long is a session?

» Is there an extra cost for any follow-up letters?

Medicare, such as OHIP in Ontario, pays only medical doctors, psychiatrists, nurse practitioners, and endocrinologists. Psychologists, psychotherapists, and social workers are private and are not paid by Medicare.

Some private insurance companies cover some of the medical costs. Find out from your insurance company what professions are covered. Ensure you receive a receipt for all expenses to include for tax deductions.

For those seeking support, a question that many people ask is: **How many sessions will I need?** This is difficult to answer since it depends on what stage you are in the transition process. Consider posing the following questions to yourself:

» Are you still questioning if you are transgender?

» Are you seeking someone to confirm a gender dysphoria diagnosis since you already know you are transgender?

» Are you seeking someone who can write the letter to start hormone treatments?

» Are you seeking a qualified person for OHIP approval and a surgery-approval letter since you have already been on HRT for one year?

For the questioning person, a few sessions might be enough, others may need more time. (Chapter 5 might answer some of your questions.) A full assessment will need to be done. As well, the eligibility and readiness criteria of the World Professional Association for Transgender Health Standards of Care and for SRS the OHIP (or your province Medicare requirements) will have to be fulfilled.

The World Professional Association for Transgender Health Standards of Care (WPAT) guidelines are generally recognized by most Medicare (such as OHIP for Ontario), endocrinologists, and plastic surgeons; however, requirements may differ depending on where you reside.

Surgery assessments (SRS) can only be done by the following practitioners:

» Physician

» Nurse Practitioner

» Registered Nurse

» Psychologist

» Registered Social Worker (Social Worker)

» **Please note:** In Ontario, an eligible psychologist or social worker must have, as a minimum, a master's degree in psychology or social work and a current and valid registration with the Association of Psychologist or the Ontario College or Social Workers and Social Service Workers.

The supporting assessment(s) must be completed by a provider, (1-5 above), trained in the assessment, diagnosis, and treatment in accordance with the World Professional Association for Transgender Health Standards of Care that are in place at the time of recommendations.

When you find a doctor to work with, you should feel very comfortable with them, and confident that you are getting all the information you need. The goal in working together with your practitioners is to move toward you living a healthy, happy life.

For further information

» World Professional Association for Transgender Health (WPATH)

» Canadian Professional Association for Transgender Health (CPATH)

» LBGTQ+ centres

» Mental ealth centres

» Community health centres

These centres can offer helpful information and can guide you in the direction you need. Also note that, increasingly, doctors, psychologists, and social workers are expanding their practice for online support. This is particularly helpful for communities without direct access to experienced practitioners.

I hope these suggestions and questions will assist you in finding the right support for living a happy and healthy life—for your own journey or for the journey of a loved one.

CHAPTER 9

Concluding Thoughts

This chapter is not so much a conclusion as it is an invitation to reflect and consider questions about your own responses to difference—gender or otherwise. Why are we so uncomfortable with difference? How can we address issues of prejudice and reduce discrimination of people who are different from us? The answers are not simple.

THOUGHTS

Concluding Thoughts

This is not a conclusion, rather a place to reflect. For those who have read each chapter, thank you for taking the time to journey through curious and perhaps unknown waters. For those who skimmed through the book and read headings and quotes for key messages, then welcome to these concluding thoughts.

Three voices have been brought together to speak with you through the writing of this book: the voice of a mother who witnessed her child shift from awkward to awesome as he claimed his confidence and gender authenticity; the voice of a gender specialist who shares her knowledge and wisdom of a thirty-year medical practice focused almost exclusively on transgender and gender-diverse people; and the voice of a young man who shares his insights about the challenging path he walked to come to terms with his discomfort in self and his journey to transition from female to male while in his early twenties. What the three of us have in common is not only our connection to the dialogue of gender questioning but also our deep dedication to inviting others into this discourse.

Many conversations have been started and woven throughout the book to accomplish three things: to help readers learn new things about the topic of gender; to invite reflection on the idea that gender is a spectrum that embraces a multitude of experiences and expressions; and to inspire you, dear reader, to consider what gender means to you—to be consciously curious about gender.

Each of us has our own relationship to the gender we were assigned at birth. How comfortable or uncomfortable we are with that gender shapes the way we relate to ourselves. If we are comfortable with our gender, there's no perceived issue. It is being *un*comfortable with our gender that leads us to seek ways to create a different, more relatable relationship with it.

As we all move through our lives, there are ideas we have that we begin to understand as things we "know." Once we know something, we can't *un*know it, though our learning never stops and our understandings and lessons may change. New information and circumstances may arise and call us to rethink what it is we know, yet throughout our life, our understandings, perspectives, judgments, and knowings continue to evolve.

You might find it worthwhile to take some time here to think about this concept of "knowing," and invite yourself to consider the relationship you have to your own gender. Consider too the subject of gender in relation to your friends, family, co-workers, community, and beyond. Do you consider gender within a confined structure shaping what is and is not "normal" or "acceptable," or do you view gender as a spectrum of identities?

Whatever is being revealed to you as you reflect on your own relationship to gender is worthy of acknowledgement. Perhaps this book has invited you into a conscious consideration of your own relationship to gender and allowing some new questions. Perhaps this book has given you new information and insights, possibly shifting you out of judgement and into curiosity about how others express their own gender.

If you are someone who had not thought a lot about their gender or ever really explored your own relationship to it, have you unearthed new understandings or curiosities of where you see yourself on the spectrum of gender?

If you found out that your neighbour, co-worker, child, parent, or partner is trans or non-binary identifying, would that change the way you interact or feel about them? How? Why?

We are all on an ever-unfolding path of learning and growing throughout life, yet we can so easily remain locked in our own unconscious biases.

As Dr. Helma wrote in her conclusion of Chapter 5, "the discussion about gender is a topic about visibility, being visible, being recognized, and accepted in the gender or genders that only you know is the right one for you. Education can help to alleviate fears, and we need to work together to achieve positive change. Then, and only then, will we be able to ensure that everyone on the gender continuum is included and is a full participant in society."

So how *can* each of us ensure that everyone on the gender continuum feels included as a full participant in society? Another way to ask this question is, "How can we address prejudice and reduce discrimination of people who are different from us?" The answer involves reviewing both our internal thoughts and our external behaviours.

To embrace people who are different from us requires that we start from our heart place:

» Be curious and aware when your judgements take over

» Be respectful—in public and in private places

» Be willing to accept difference

» Be willing to explore a broader concept of gender.

Active support can look many ways:

» Seek out information to expand your understanding (as you are now doing here)

» Support laws and regulations that require fair and equal treatment for all groups of people

» Participate in public-support activities to bring awareness against discrimination

» Help those around you become more open to difference.

Throughout this book, many questions have been posed to invite your own reflections about the various ideas and insights that have been shared. My final question seeks to go beyond the ideas of gender difference and ask what I consider to be a key question for us all: **"Why does difference make us so uncomfortable?"**

A behaviouralist might say that "there is a tendency to devalue things and people that are different. Human beings seem to have a strong penchant for a 'difference equals deficiency' bias. In other words, anything that is different or strange is seen as being less good than things that are familiar."[34]

A neuroscientist might say that we are much like our evolutionary ancestors, groomed to protect ourselves against threat. Our brain is fitted with an amygdala (actually two: one on each side of the brain) that has been referred to as "the brain's smoke detector."[35] It has many jobs, including storing memories and emotions, but it's most known for alerting the brain and body to a possible emergency. How it does this is by sussing out things that are different, unexpected, and unfamiliar, and translating that recognition into a fight-flight-fear-freeze set of responses. That might mean any number of behaviours from passive avoidance to aggressive attacking.

....

34 "Resistance to Multiculturalism, Issues and Interventions" by Jeffrey Scott Mio and Gene I. Awakuni

35 "The Body Keeps the Score" by Dr. Bessel Van Der Kolk

Given these ideas about common responses to difference, my invitation—and perhaps even my call to action—is this: When you feel yourself experiencing mental or physical discomfort in the presence of someone who is different from you, be that in their gender expression, sexual orientation, colour, race, religion, age, style of clothing, or myriad other ways people are different from one another, ask yourself:

"Why is this a problem?"

Whatever answer you come up with, continue to ask yourself:
"Why is this a problem?"

Continue asking yourself this one question until you feel you are at the heart of your own biases. I invite you to sit with this and let yourself be with it.

Now ask yourself:
"How do I want to proceed with this situation / person / perception now?"

My hope is that you will use your increased information and self-awareness to contribute to a world that is kinder, gentler, and more supportive of each other. My hope is that you will be an ally to those who are different from you. Embracing difference starts in the heart. It emanates out easily once the glow has begun. Changing the world *is* possible, one heart glow at a time.

AUTHORS

About the Authors

Suzanne Sherkin

Suzanne is the proud mother of two children, her daughter Lauren and her son Skyler who transitioned from female to male in his early twenties. A Qualified Mediator, her Toronto-based practice addresses issues of conflict, harassment, and stigma in workplaces across Canada. Suzanne has spoken at numerous conferences on the topics of 'The Neuroscience of Conflict,' 'Unconscious Bias in Mediation,' and 'Gender Diversity in the Workplace.' A former editor of national magazines in Canada, this is Suzanne's first published book. She rides a Harley to maintain balance in mind, body, and spirit.

Dr. Helma Seidl, PhD, MSW, RSW, Psychotherapist

Dr Seidl graduated from McGill University with a PhD in Social Work. She also has an MSW from McGill University; BSW McGill University; B.A. Arts Honours Psychology, Carleton University, Ottawa, Ontario; Registered Nursing Degree, Nursing College, University Clinic, Innsbruck, Austria; Head-Nurse Degree, Nursing College, University Clinic, Innsbruck, Austria; PTSD training and Eye movement desensitization and reprocessing (EMDR) certification.

She works in private practice as a Gender Specialist (transgender issues), providing direct services to clients who are dealing with transgender issues: transitioning or fluidity. Public presentations include McGill University, Queens University, Ottawa University, Heritage College, and Algonquin College to sensitize social workers, doctors, sociology and law students to examine their personal attitudes and beliefs, and understand gender, sexual, cultural, and social issues when working with the LGBTQ+ community.

She has presented at the Annual Conference for the Canadian Psychiatry Association: Transgenderism: Part of a Greater Gender Continuum or Pathology? She has also presented at the Annual Conference for the Canadian Professional Association for Transgender Health: Improving Inclusiveness in Transgender Counselling; Transgender: A study on quality of life. She has given presentations at many hospitals on transgender, and is on Youtube: Help for the trans community and families with CHEO.

Dr. Seidl's published works include:

Seidl, H. (2008). *Transgenderism: a quantitative and qualitative study.* Unpublished PhD Thesis, McGill University, Montreal, Canada.

Seidl, H. (2006). Transgenderism: Part of a Greater Gender Continuum or Pathology? In Augustine Meier & Martin Rovers (Eds.), *Through Conflict to Reconciliation (pp.189-212).* Saint Paul University, Ottawa, Ontario: Novalis Publisher.

Seidl, H. (2002). *Counsellor/Therapist Educational Knowledge and Qualification Survey.* Unpublished research paper, McGill University, Montreal, Canada.

Seidl, H. (2000). *Post-Traumatic Stress Disorder Associated with Transgenderism and "Self-Identity" Re-Formation.* Unpublished Master's Thesis, McGill University, Montreal, Canada.

Skyler Hagen

Skyler has a practice as a Mental Health Counselor and is in the process of becoming an accredited practitioner in Alternative Dispute Resolution (ADR). He is a visual artist who has exhibited his work across Canada. He embraces the power of curiosity to keep his heart open and his spirit creative. Skyler currently lives in Toronto with his girlfriend and cat.